Theodore Roosevelt
America and the First World War.
Collected Essays

AF131826

SEVERUS Verlag

Roosevelt. Theodore: America and the First World War. Collected Essays. 2020
Neuauflage der Ausgabe von 1920
ISBN: 978-3-96345-091-4

Korrektorat: Lisa Seidelt
Satz: Lisa Seidelt

Umschlaggestaltung: Annelie Lamers, SEVERUS Verlag
Umschlagmotiv: www.pixabay.com

Bibliografische Information der Deutschen Nationalbibliothek: Die Deutsche Nationalbibliothek verzeichnet diese Publikation in der Deutschen Nationalbibliografie; detaillierte bibliografische Daten sind im Internet über https://dnb.de abrufbar.

Der SEVERUS Verlag ist ein Imprint der Bedey & Thoms Media GmbH, Hermannstal 119k, 22119 Hamburg

_____

SEVERUS Verlag, 2020
http://www.severus-verlag.de
Gedruckt in Deutschland
Der SEVERUS Verlag übernimmt keine juristische Verantwortung oder irgendeine Haftung für evtl. fehlerhafte Angaben und deren Folgen.

Theodore Roosevelt

America and the First World War

Collected Essays

Editorische Notiz:
Der Text der vorliegenden Edition beruht auf der Ausgabe:
Theodore Roosevelt: America and the First World War. 6. Auflage, New York 1920. Die Or-
thographie wurde behutsam modernisiert, grammatikalische Eigenheiten bleiben ge-
wahrt. Die Interpunktion folgt der Druckvorlage. Der Inhalt ist im historischen Kontext zu
lesen.

Inhalt

Prayer for Peace

Now these were visions in the night of war:

I prayed for peace; God, answering my prayer,
Sent down a grievous plague on humankind,
A black and tumorous plague that softly slew
Till nations and their armies were no more –
   And there was perfect peace …
But I awoke, wroth with high God and prayer.

I prayed for peace; God, answering my prayer,
Decreed the Truce of Life: – Wings in the sky
Fluttered and fell; the quick, bright ocean things
Sank to the ooze; the footprints in the woods
Vanished; the freed brute from the abattoir
Starved on green pastures; and within the blood
The death-work at the root of living ceased;
And men gnawed clods and stones, blasphemed and died—
   And there was perfect peace …
But I awoke, wroth with high God and prayer.

I prayed for peace; God, answering my prayer,
Bowed the free neck beneath a yoke of steel,
Dumbed the free voice that springs in lyric speech,
Killed the free art that glows on all mankind,
And made one iron nation lord of earth,
Which in the monstrous matrix of its will
Moulded a spawn of slaves. There was One Might –
And there was perfect peace …
But I awoke, wroth with high God and prayer.

I prayed for peace; God, answering my prayer,
Palsied all flesh with bitter fear of death.
The shuddering slayers fled to town and field

Beset with carrion visions, foul decay,
And sickening taints of air that made the earth
One charnel of the shrivelled lines of war.
And through all flesh that omnipresent fear
Became the strangling fingers of a hand
That choked aspiring thought and brave belief
And love of loveliness and selfless deed
Till flesh was all, flesh wallowing, styed in fear,
In festering fear that stank beyond the stars –
    And there was perfect peace ...
But I awoke, wroth with high God and prayer.

I prayed for peace; God, answering my prayer,
Spake very softly of forgotten things,
Spake very softly old remembered words
Sweet as young starlight. Rose to heaven again
The mystic challenge of the Nazarene,
That deathless affirmation: – Man in God
And God in man willing the God to be ...
And there was war and peace, and peace and war,
Full year and lean, joy, anguish, life and death,
Doing their work on the evolving soul,
The soul of man in God and God in man.
For death is nothing in the sum of things,
And life is nothing in the sum of things,
And flesh is nothing in the sum of things,
But man in God is all and God in man,
Will merged in will, love immanent in love,
Moving through visioned vistas to one goal –
The goal of man in God and God in man,
And of all life in God and God in life –
The far fruition of our earthly prayer,
"Thy will be done!" ... There is no other peace!

William Samuel Jonson.

Foreword

In the New York *Evening* Post for September 30, 1814, a correspondent writes from Washington that on the ruins of the Capitol, which had just been burned by a small British army, various disgusted patriots had written sentences which included the following: "Fruits of war without preparation" and "Mirror of democracy." A century later, in December, 1914, the same paper, ardently championing the policy of national unpreparedness and claiming that democracy was incompatible with preparedness against war, declared that it was moved to tears by its pleasure in the similar championship of the same policy contained in President Wilson's just-published message to Congress. The message is for the most part couched in terms of adroit and dexterous, and usually indirect, suggestion, and carefully avoids downright, or indeed straightforward, statement of policy – the meaning being conveyed in questions and hints, often so veiled and so obscure as to make it possible to draw contradictory conclusions from the words used. There are, however, fairly clear statements that we are "not to depend upon a standing army nor yet upon a reserve army," nor upon any efficient system of universal training for our young men, but upon vague and unformulated plans for encouraging volunteer aid for militia service by making it "as attractive as possible"! The message contains such sentences as that the President "hopes" that "some of the finer passions" of the American people "are in his own heart"; that "dread of the power of any other nation we are incapable of"; such sentences as, shall we "be prepared to defend ourselves against attack? We have always found means to do that, and shall find them whenever it is necessary," and "if asked, are you ready to defend yourself? we reply, most assuredly, to the utmost." It is difficult for a serious and patriotic citizen to understand how the President could have been willing to make such statements as these. Every student even of elementary American history knows that in our last foreign war with a formidable opponent, that of 1812, reliance on the principles President Wilson now advocates brought us to the verge of national ruin and of the break-up of the Union. The President must know that at that time we had not "found means" even to defend the capital city in which he was writing his message. He ought to know that at the present time, thanks largely to his own actions, we are not "ready to defend ourselves" at all, not to speak of defending ourselves "to the utmost." In a state paper subtle prettiness of phrase does not offset misteaching of the vital facts of national history.

In 1814 this nation was paying for its folly in having for fourteen years conducted its foreign policy, and refused to prepare for defense against possible foreign foes, in accordance with the views of the ultra-pacificists of that day. It behooves us now, in the presence of a world war even vaster and more terrible than the world war of the early nineteenth century, to beware of taking the advice of the equally foolish pacificists of our own day. To follow their advice at the present time might expose our democracy to far greater disaster than was brought upon it by its disregard of Washington's maxim, and its failure to secure peace by preparing against war, a hundred years ago.

In his message President Wilson has expressed his laudable desire that this country, naturally through its President, may act as mediator to bring peace among the great European powers. With this end in view he, in his message, deprecates our taking any efficient steps to prepare means for our own defense, lest such action might give a wrong impression to the great warring powers. Furthermore, in his overanxiety not to offend the powerful who have done wrong, he scrupulously refrains from saying one word on behalf of the weak who have suffered wrong. He makes no allusion to the violation of the Hague conventions at Belgium's expense, although this nation had solemnly undertaken to be a guarantor of those conventions. He makes no protest against the cruel wrongs Belgium has suffered. He says not one word about the need, in the interests of true peace, of the only peace worth having, that steps should be taken to prevent the repetition of such wrongs in the future.

This is not right. It is not just to the weaker nations of the earth. It comes perilously near a betrayal of our own interests. In his laudable anxiety to make himself acceptable as a mediator to England, and especially to Germany, President Wilson loses sight of the fact that his first duty is to the United States; and, moreover, desirable though it is that his conduct should commend him to Germany, to England, and to the other great contending powers, he should not for this reason forget the interests of the small nations, and above all of Belgium, whose gratitude never mean anything tangible to him or to us, but which has suffered a wrong that in any peace negotiations it should be our first duty to see remedied.

In the following chapters, substantially reproduced from articles contributed to the Wheeler Syndicate and also to *The Outlook*, *The Independent*, and *Everybody's*, the attempt is made to draw from the present lamentable contest certain lessons which it would be well for our people to learn. Among them are the following:

We, a people akin to and yet different from all the peoples of Europe, should be equally friendly to all these peoples while they behave well, should be courteous to and considerate of the rights of each of them, but should not hesitate to judge each and all of them by their conduct.

The kind of "neutrality" which seeks to preserve "peace" by timidly refusing to live up to our plighted word and to denounce and take action against such wrong as that committed in the case of Belgium, is unworthy of an honorable and powerful people. Dante reserved a special place of infamy in the inferno for those base angels who dared side neither with evil nor with good. Peace is ardently to be desired, but only as the handmaid of righteousness. The only peace of permanent value is the peace of righteousness. There can be no such peace until well-behaved, highly civilized small nations are protected from oppression and subjugation.

National promises, made in treaties, in Hague conventions, and the like are like the promises of individuals. The sole value of the promise comes in the performance. Recklessness in making promises is in practice almost or quite as mischievous and dishonest as indifference to keeping promises; and this as much in the case of nations as in the case of individuals. Upright men make few promises, and keep those they make.

All the actions of the ultrapacificists for a generation past, all their peace congresses and peace conventions, have amounted to precisely and exactly nothing in advancing the cause of peace. The peace societies of the ordinary pacificist type have in the aggregate failed to accomplish even the smallest amount of good, have done nothing whatever for peace, and the very small effect they have had on their own nations has been, on the whole, slightly detrimental. Although usually they have been too futile to be even detrimental, their unfortunate tendency has so far been to make good men weak and to make virtue a matter of derision to strong men. All-inclusive arbitration treaties of the kind hitherto proposed and enacted are utterly worthless, are hostile righteousness and detrimental to peace. The Americans, within and without Congress, who have opposed the fortifying of the Panama Canal and the up-building of the American navy have been false to the honor and the interest of the nation and should be condemned by every high-minded citizen.

In every serious crisis the present Hague conventions and the peace and arbitration and neutrality treaties of the existing type have proved not to be worth the paper on which they were written. This is because no method was provided of securing their enforcement, of putting force behind the pledge. Peace treaties and arbitration treaties unbacked by force are not merely useless but mischievous in any serious crisis.

Treaties must never be recklessly made; improper treaties should be repudiated long before the need for action under them arises; and all treaties not thus repudiated in advance should be scrupulously kept.

From the international standpoint the essential thing to do is effectively to put the combined power of civilization back of the collective purpose of civilization to secure justice. This can be achieved only by a world league for the peace of righteousness, which would guarantee to enforce by the combined strength of all the nations the decrees of a competent and impartial court against any recalcitrant and offending nation. Only in this way will treaties become serious documents.

Such a world league for peace is not now in sight. Until it is created the prime necessity for each free and liberty-loving nation is to keep itself in such a state of efficient preparedness as to be able to defend by its own strength both its honor and its vital interest. The most important lesson for the United States to learn from the present war is the vital need that it shall at once take steps thus to prepare.

Preparedness against war does not always avert war or disaster in war any more than the existence of a fire department, that is, of preparedness against fire, always averts fire. But it is the only insurance against war and the only insurance against overwhelming disgrace and disaster in war. Preparedness usually averts war and usually prevents disaster in war; and always prevents disgrace in war. Preparedness, so far from encouraging nations to go to war, has a marked tendency to diminish the chance of war occurring. Unpreparedness has not the slightest effect in averting war. Its only effect is immensely to increase the likelihood of disgrace and disaster in war. The United States should immediately strengthen its navy and provide for its steady training in purely military functions; it should similarly strengthen the regular army and provide a reserve; and, furthermore, it should provide for all the young men of the nation military training of the kind practised by the free democracy of Switzerland. Switzerland is the least "militaristic" and most democratic of republics, and the best prepared against war. If we follow her example we will be carrying out the precepts of Washington.

We feel no hostility toward any nation engaged in the present tremendous struggle. We feel an infinite sadness because of the black abyss of war into which all these nations have been plunged. We admire the heroism they have shown. We act in a spirit of warm friendliness toward all of them, even when obliged to protest against the wrong-doing of any one of them.

Our country should not shirk its duty to mankind. It can perform this duty only if it is true to itself. It can be true to itself only by definitely resolving to take the position of the just man armed; for a proud and self-respecting nation of freemen must scorn to do wrong to others and must also scorn tamely to submit to wrong done by others.

Theodore Roosevelt.

Sagamore Hill,

January 1, 1915.

Chapter I

THE DUTY OF SELF-DEFENSE AND
OF GOOD CONDUCT TOWARD OTHERS

In this country we are both shocked and stunned by the awful catac-lysm which has engulfed civilized Europe. By only a few men was the possibility of such a wide-spread and hideous disaster even admit-ted. Most persons, even after it occurred, felt as if it was unbelievable. They felt that in what it pleased enthusiasts to speak of as "this age of enlightenment" it was impossible that primal passion, working hand in hand with the most modern scientific organization, should loose upon the world these forces of dread destruction.

In the last week in July the men and women of the populous civi-lized countries of Europe were leading their usual ordered lives, busy and yet soft, lives carried on with comfort and luxury, with appliances for ease and pleasure such as never before were known, lives led in a routine which to most people seemed part of the natural order of things, something which could not be disturbed by shocks such as the world knew of old. A fortnight later hell yawned under the feet of these hard-working or pleasure-seeking men and women, and woe smote them as it smote the peoples we read of in the Old Testament or in the histories of the Middle Ages. Through the rents in our smiling surface of civilization the volcanic fires beneath gleamed red in the gloom.

What occurred in Europe is on a giant scale like the disaster to the *Titanic*. One moment the great ship was speeding across the ocean, equipped with every device for comfort, safety, and luxury. The men in her stoke-hold and steerage were more comfortable than the most luxurious travellers of a century ago. The people in her first-class cabins enjoyed every luxury that a luxurious city life could demand and were screened not only from danger but from the least discomfort or annoyance. Suddenly, in one awful and shattering moment, death smote the floating host, so busy with work and play. They were in that moment shot back through immeasurable ages. At one stroke they were hurled from a life of effortless ease back into elemental disaster; to disaster in which baseness showed naked, and heroism burned like a flame of light.

In the face of a calamity so world-wide as the present war, it behooves us all to keep our heads clear and to read aright the lessons taught us; far we ourselves may suffer dreadful penalties if we read these lessons wrong. The temptation always is only to half-learn such a lesson, for a half-truth is always simple, whereas the whole truth is very, very difficult. Unfortunately, a half-truth, if applied, may turn out to be the most dangerous type of falsehood.

Now, our business here in America in the face of this cataclysm is twofold. In the first place it is imperative that we shall take the steps necessary in order, by our own strength and wisdom, to safeguard ourselves against such disaster as has occurred in Europe. Events have shown that peace treaties, arbitration treaties, neutrality treaties, Hague treaties, and the like as at present existing, offer not even the smallest protection against such disasters. The prime duty of the moment is therefore to keep Uncle Sam in such a position that by his own stout heart and ready hand he can defend the vital honor and vital interest of the American people.

But this is not our only duty, even although it is the only duty we can immediately perform. The horror of what has occurred in Europe, which has drawn into the maelstrom of war large parts of Asia, Africa, Australasia, and even America, is altogether too great to permit us to rest supine without endeavoring to prevent its repetition. We are not to be excused if we do not make a resolute and intelligent effort to devise some scheme which will minimize the chance for a recurrence of such horror in the future and which will at least limit and alleviate it if it should occur. In other words, it is our duty to try to devise some efficient plan for securing the peace of righteousness throughout the world.

That any plan will surely and automatically bring peace we cannot promise. Nevertheless, I think a plan can be devised which will render it far more difficult than at present to plunge us into a world war and far more easy than at present to find workable and practical substitutes even for ordinary war. In order to do this, however, it is necessary that we shall fearlessly look facts in the face. We cannot devise methods for securing peace which will actually work unless we are in good faith willing to face the fact that the present all-inclusive arbitration treaties, peace conferences, and the like, upon which our well-meaning pacifists have pinned so much hope, have proved utterly worthless under serious strain. We must face this fact and clearly understand the reason for it before we can advance an adequate remedy.

It is even more important not to pay heed to the pathetic infatuation of the well-meaning persons who declare that this is "the last great war." During the last century such assertions have been made again and again after the close of every great war. They represent nothing but an amiable fatuity. The strong men of the United States must protect the feeble; but they must not trust for guidance to the feeble.

In these chapters I desire to ask my fellow countrymen and countrywomen to consider the various lessons which are being writ in letters of blood and steel before our eyes. I wish to ask their consideration, first, of the immediate need that we shall realize the utter hopelessness under actually existing conditions of our trusting for our safety merely to the good-will of other powers or to treaties or other "bits of paper" or to anything except our own steadfast courage and preparedness. Second, I wish to point out what a complicated and difficult thing it is to work for peace and how difficult it may be to combine doing one's duty in the endeavor to bring peace for others without failing in one's duty to secure peace for one's self; and therefore I wish to point out how unwise it is to make foolish promises which under great strain it would be impossible to keep.

Third, I wish to try to give practical expression to what I know is the hope of the great body of our people. We should endeavor to devise some method of action, in common with other nations, whereby there shall be at least a reasonable chance of securing world peace and, in any event, of narrowing the sphere of possible war and its horrors. To do this it is equally necessary unflinchingly to antagonize the position of the men who believe in nothing but brute force exercised without regard to the rights of other nations, and unhesitatingly to condemn the well-meaning but unwise persons who seek to mislead our people into the belief that treaties, mere bits of paper, when unbacked by force and when there is no one responsible for their enforcement, can be of the slightest use in a serious crisis. Force unbacked by righteousness is abhorrent. The effort to substitute for it vague declamation for righteousness unbacked by force is silly. The policeman must be put back of the judge in international law just as he is back of the judge in municipal law. The effective power of civilization must be put back of civilization's collective purpose to secure reasonable justice between nation and nation.

First, consider the lessons taught by this war as to the absolute need under existing conditions of our being willing, ready, and able to defend ourselves from unjust attack. What has befallen Belgium and Luxembourg – not to speak of China – during the past five months shows the utter hopelessness of trusting to any treaties, no matter how well meant, unless back of them lies power sufficient to secure their enforcement.

At the outset let me explain with all possible emphasis that in what I am about to say at this time I am not criticising nor taking sides with any one of the chief combatants in either group of warring powers, so far as the relations between and among these chief powers themselves are concerned. The causes for the present contest stretch into the immemorial past. As far as the present generations of Germans, Frenchmen, Russians, Austrians, and Serbians are concerned, their actions have been determined by deeds done and left undone by many generations in the past. Not only the sovereigns but the peoples engaged on each side believe sincerely in the justice of their several causes. This is convincingly shown by the action of the Socialists in Germany, France, and Belgium. Of all latter-day political parties the Socialist is the one in which international brotherhood is most dwelt upon, while international obligations are placed on a par with national obligations. Yet the Socialists in Germany and the Socialists in France and Belgium have all alike thrown themselves into this contest with the same enthusiasm and, indeed, the same bitterness as the rest of their countrymen. I am not at this moment primarily concerned with passing judgment upon any of the powers. I am merely instancing certain things that have occurred, because of the vital importance that we as a people should take to heart the lessons taught by these occurrences.

At the end of July Belgium and Luxembourg were independent nations. By treaties executed in 1832 and 1867 their neutrality had been guaranteed by the great nations round about them – Germany, France, and England. Their neutrality was thus guaranteed with the express purpose of keeping them at peace and preventing any invasion of their territory during war. Luxembourg built no fortifications and raised no army, trusting entirely to the pledged faith of her neighbors. Belgium, an extremely thrifty, progressive, and prosperous industrial country, whose people are exceptionally hard-working and law-abiding, raised an army and built forts for purely defensive purposes. Neither nation committed the smallest act of hostility or aggression against any one of its neighbors. Each behaved with absolute propriety. Each was absolutely innocent of the slightest wrong-doing. Neither has the very smallest responsibility for the disaster that has overwhelmed her. Nevertheless as soon as the war broke out the territories of both were overrun.

Luxembourg made no resistance. It is now practically incorporated in Germany. Other nations have almost forgotten its existence and not the slightest attention has been paid to its fate simply because it did not fight, simply because it trusted solely to peaceful measures and to the treaties which were supposed to guarantee it against harm. The eyes of the world, however, are on Belgium because the Belgians have fought hard and gallantly for all that makes life best worth having to honorable men and women. In consequence, Belgium has been trampled under foot. At this moment not only her men but her women and children are enduring misery so dreadful that it is hard for us who live at peace to visualize it to ourselves.

The fate of Luxembourg and of Belgium offers an instructive commentary on the folly of the well-meaning people who a few years ago insisted that the Panama Canal should not be fortified and that we should trust to international treaties to protect it. After what has occurred in Europe no sane man has any excuse for believing that such treaties would avail us in our hour of need any more than they have availed Belgium and Luxembourg – and, for that matter, Korea and China – in their hours of need.

If a great world war should arise or if a great world-power were at war with us under conditions that made it desirable for other nations not to be drawn into the quarrel, any step that the hostile nation's real or fancied need demanded would unquestionably be taken, and any treaty that stood in the way would be treated as so much waste paper except so far as we could back it by force. If under such circumstances Panama is retained and controlled by us, it will be because our forts and garrison and our fleets on the ocean make it unsafe to meddle with the canal and the canal zone. Were it only protected by a treaty – that is, unless behind the treaty lay both force and the readiness to use force – the canal would not be safe for twenty-four hours. Moreover, in such case, the real blame would lie at our own doors. We would not be helped at all, we would merely make ourselves objects of derision, if under these circumstances we screamed and clamored about the iniquity of those who violated the treaty and took possession of Panama. The blame would rightly be placed by the world upon our own supine folly, upon our own timidity and weakness, and we would be adjudged unfit to hold what we had shown ourselves too soft and too short-sighted to retain.

The most obvious lesson taught by what has occurred is the utter worthlessness of treaties unless backed by force. It is evident that as things are now, all-inclusive arbitration treaties, neutrality treaties, treaties of alliance, and the like do not serve one particle of good in protecting a peaceful nation when some great military power deems its vital needs at stake, unless the rights of this peaceful nation are backed by force. The devastation of Belgium, the burning of Louvain, the holding of Brussels to heavy ransom, the killing of women and children, the wrecking of houses in Antwerp by bombs from air-ships have excited genuine sympathy among neutral nations. But no neutral nation has protested; and while unquestionably a neutral nation like the United States ought to have protested, yet the only certain way to make such a protest effective would be to put force back of it. Let our people remember that what has been done to Belgium would unquestionably be done to us by any great military power with which we were drawn into war, no matter how just our cause. Moreover, it would be done without any more protest on the part of neutral nations than we have ourselves made in the case of Belgium.

If, as an aftermath of this war, some great Old-World power or combination of powers made war on us because we objected to their taking and fortifying Magdalena Bay or St. Thomas, our chance of securing justice would rest exclusively on the efficiency of our fleet and army, especially the fleet. No arbitration treaties, or peace treaties, of the kind recently negotiated at Washington by the bushelful, and no tepid good-will of neutral powers, would help us in even the smallest degree. If our fleet were conquered, New York and San Francisco would be seized and probably each would be destroyed as Louvain was destroyed unless it were put to ransom as Brussels has been put to ransom. Under such circumstances outside powers would undoubtedly remain neutral exactly as we have remained neutral as regards Belgium.

Under such conditions my own view is very strongly that the national interest would be best served by refusing the payment of all ransom and accepting the destruction of the cities and then continuing the war until by our own strength and indomitable will we had exacted ample atonement from our foes. This would be a terrible price to pay for unpreparedness; and those responsible for the unpreparedness would thereby be proved guilty of a crime against the nation. Upon them would rest the guilt of all the blood and misery. The innocent would have to atone for their folly and strong men would have to undo and offset it by submitting to the destruction of our cities rather than consent to save them by paying money which would be used to prosecute the war against the rest of the country. If our people are wise and far-sighted and if they still have in their blood the iron of the men who fought under Grant and Lee, they will, in the event of such a war, insist upon this price being paid, upon this course being followed. They will then in the end exact, from the nation which assails us, atonement for the misery and redress for the wrong done. They will not rely upon the ineffective good-will of neutral outsiders. They will show a temper that will make our foes think twice before meddling with us again.

The great danger to peace so far as this country is concerned arises from such pacificists as those who have made and applauded our recent all-inclusive arbitration treaties, who advocate the abandonment of our policy of building battleships and the refusal to fortify the Panama Canal. It is always possible that these persons may succeed in impressing foreign nations with the belief that they represent our people. If they ever do succeed in creating this conviction in the minds of other nations, the fate of the United States will speedily be that of China and Luxembourg, or else it will be saved therefrom only by long-drawn war, accompanied by incredible bloodshed and disaster.

It is those among us who would go to the front in such event – as I and my four sons would go – who are the really far-sighted and earnest friends of peace. We desire measures taken in the real interest of peace because we, who at need would fight, but who earnestly hope never to be forced to fight, have most at stake in keeping peace. We object to the actions of those who do most talking about the necessity of peace because we think they are really a menace to the just and honorable peace which alone this country will in the long run support. We object to their actions because we believe they represent a course of conduct which may at any time produce a war in which we and not they would labor and suffer.

In such a war the prime fact to be remembered is that the men really responsible for it would not be those who would pay the penalty. The ultrapacificists are rarely men who go to battle. Their fault or their folly would be expiated by the blood of countless thousands of plain and decent American citizens of the stamp of those, North and South alike, who in the Civil War laid down all they had, including life itself, in battling for the right as it was given to them to see the right.

Chapter II

THE BELGIAN TRAGEDY

Peace is worthless unless it serves the cause of righteousness. Peace which consecrates militarism is of small service. Peace obtained by crushing the liberty and life of just and unoffending peoples is as cruel as the most cruel war. It should ever be our honorable effort to serve one of the world's most vital needs by doing all in our power to bring about conditions which will give some effective protection to weak or small nations which themselves keep order and act with justice toward the rest of mankind. There can be no higher international duty than to safeguard the existence and independence of industrious, orderly states, with a high personal and national standard of conduct, but without the military force of the great powers; states, for instance, such as Belgium, Holland, Switzerland, the Scandinavian countries, Uruguay, and others. A peace which left Belgium's wrongs unredressed and which did not provide against the recurrence of such wrongs as those from which she has suffered would not be a real peace.

As regards the actions of most of the combatants in the hideous world-wide war now raging it is possible sincerely to take and defend either of the opposite views concerning their actions. The causes of any such great and terrible contest almost always lie far back in the past, and the seeming immediate cause is usually itself in major part merely an effect of many preceding causes The assassination of the heir to the Austro-Hungarian throne was partly or largely due to the existence of political and often murderous secret societies in Serbia which the Serbian government did not suppress; and it did not suppress them because the "bondage" of the men and women of the Serbian race in Bosnia and Herzegovina to Austria was such a source of ever-present irritation to the Serbians that their own government was powerless to restrain them. Strong arguments can be advanced on both the Austrian and the Serbian sides as regards this initial cause of the present world-wide war.

Again, when once the war was started between Austria and Serbia, it can well be argued that it was impossible for Russia not to take part. Had she not done so, she would have forfeited her claims to the leadership of the smaller Slav peoples; and the leading Russian liberals enthusiastically support the Russian government in this matter, asserting that Russia's triumph in this particular struggle means a check to militarism, a stride toward greater freedom, and an advance in justice toward the Pole, the Jew, the Finn, and the people of the Caucasus.

When Russia took part it may well be argued that it was impossible for Germany not to come to the defense of Austria, and that disaster would surely have attended her arms had she not followed the course she actually did follow as regards her opponents on her western frontier. As for her wonderful efficiency – her equipment, the foresight and decision of her General Staff, her instantaneous action, her indomitable persistence – there can be nothing but the praise and admiration due a stern, virile, and masterful people, a people entitled to hearty respect for their patriotism and far-seeing self-devotion.

Yet again, it is utterly impossible to see how France could have acted otherwise than as she did act. She had done nothing to provoke the crisis, even although it be admitted that in the end she was certain to side with Russia. War was not declared by her, but against her, and she could not have escaped it save by having pursued in the past, and by willingness to pursue in the future, a course which would have left her as helpless as Luxembourg – and Luxembourg's fate shows that helplessness does not offer the smallest guarantee of peace.

When once Belgium was invaded, every circumstance of national honor and interest forced England to act precisely as she did act. She could not have held up her head among nations had she acted otherwise. In particular, she is entitled to the praise of all true lovers of peace, for it is only by action such as she took that neutrality treaties and treaties guaranteeing the rights of small powers will ever be given any value. The actions of Sir Edward Grey as he guided Britain's foreign policy showed adherence to lofty standards of right combined with firmness of courage under great strain. The British position, and incidentally the German position, are tersely stated in the following extract from the report of Sir Edward Goschen, who at the outset of the war was British ambassador in Berlin. The report, in speaking of the interview the ambassador and the German imperial chancellor, Herr von Bethmann-Hollweg, says:

> The chancellor [spoke] about twenty minutes. He said the step taken by Great Britain was terrible to a degree. Just for a word, "neutrality," a word which in war time had been so often disregarded, just for a scrap of paper, Great Britain was going to make war on a kindred nation. What we had done was unthinkable. It was like striking a man from behind while he was fighting for his life against two assailants. I protested strongly against this statement, and said that in the same way as he wished me to understand that for strategical reasons it was a matter of life or death to Germany to advance through Belgium and violate the latter's neutrality, so I would wish him to understand that it was, so to speak, a matter of life or death for the honor of Great Britain that she should keep her solemn engagement to do her utmost to defend Belgium's neutrality if attacked. A solemn compact simply had to be kept, or what confidence could any one have in England's engagement in the future?

There is one nation, however, as to which there is no room for difference of opinion, whether we consider her wrongs or the justice of her actions. It seems to me impossible that any man can fail to feel the deepest sympathy with a nation which is absolutely guiltless of any wrong-doing, which has given proof of high valor, and yet which has suffered terribly, and which, if there is any meaning in the words "right" and "wrong," has suffered wrongfully. Belgium is not in the smallest degree responsible for any of the conditions that during the last half century have been at work to impress a certain fatalistic stamp upon those actions of Austria, Russia, Germany, and France which have rendered this war inevitable. No European nation has had anything whatever to fear from Belgium. There was not the smallest danger of her making any aggressive movement, not even the slightest aggressive movement, against any one of her neighbors. Her population was mainly industrial and was absorbed in peaceful business. Her people were thrifty, hard-working, highly civilized, and in no way aggressive. She owed her national existence to the desire to create an absolutely neutral state. Her neutrality had been solemnly guaranteed by the great powers, including Germany as well as England and France.

Suddenly, and out of a clear sky, her territory was invaded by an overwhelming German army. According to the newspaper reports, it was admitted in the Reichstag by German members that this act was "wrongful." Of course, if time is any meaning to the words "right" and "wrong" in international matters, the act was wrong. The men who shape German policy take the ground that in matters of vital national moment there are no such things as abstract right and wrong, and that when a great nation is struggling for its existence it can no more consider the rights of neutral powers than it can consider the rights of its own citizens as these rights are construed in times of peace, and that everything must bend before the supreme law of national self-preservation. Whatever we may think of the morality of this plea, it is certain that almost all great nations have in time past again and again acted in accordance with it. England's conduct toward Denmark in the Napoleonic wars, and the conduct of both England and France toward us during those same wars, admit only of this species of justification; and with less excuse the same is true of our conduct toward Spain in Florida nearly a century ago. Nevertheless we had hoped by the action taken at The Hague to mark an advance in international morality in such matters. The action taken by Germany toward Belgium, and the failure by the United States in any way to protest against such action, shows that there has been no advance. I wish to point out just what was done, and to emphasize Belgium's absolute innocence and the horrible suffering and disaster that have overwhelmed her in spite of such innocence. And I wish to do this so that we as a nation may learn might the lessons taught by the dreadful Belgian tragedy.

Germany's attack on Belgium was not due to any sudden impulse. It had been carefully planned for a score of years, on the assumption that the treaty of neutrality was, as Herr von Bethmann-Hollweg observed, nothing but "paper," and that the question of breaking or keeping it was to be considered solely from the standpoint of Germany's interest.

The German railways up to the Belgian border are for the most part military roads, which have been double-tracked with a view to precisely the overwhelming attack that has just been delivered into and through Belgium. The great German military text-books, such as that of Bernhardi, in discussing and studying possible German campaigns against Russia and France, have treated advances through Belgium or Switzerland exactly as they have treated possible advances through German territory, it being assumed by the writers and by all for whom they wrote that no efficient rulers or military men would for a second consider a neutrality treaty or any other kind of treaty if it became to the self-interest of a party to break it. It must be remembered that the German system in no way limits its disregard of conventions to disregard of neutrality treaties. For example, in General von Bernhardi's book, in speaking of naval warfare, he lays down the following rule: "Sometimes in peace even, if there is no other means of defending one's self against a superior force, it will be advisable to attack the enemy by torpedo and submarine boats, and to inflict upon him unexpected losses … War upon the enemy's trade must also be conducted as ruthlessly as possible, since only then, in addition to the material damage inflicted upon the enemy, the necessary terror is spread among the merchant marine, which is even more important than the capture of actual prizes. A certain amount of terrorism must be practised on the sea, making peaceful tradesmen stay in safe harbors."

Belgium has felt the full effect of the practical application of these principles, and Germany has profited by them exactly as her statesmen and soldiers believed she would profit. They have believed that the material gain of trampling on Belgium would more than offset any material opposition which the act would arouse, and they treat with the utter and contemptuous derision which it deserves the mere pacifist clamor against wrong which is unaccompanied by the intention and effort to redress wrong by force.

The Belgians, when invaded, valiantly defended themselves. They acted precisely as Andreas Hofer and his Tyrolese, and Koerner and the leaders of the North German Tugendbund acted in their day; and their fate has been the fate of Andreas Hofer, who was shot after his capture, and of Koerner, who was shot in battle. They fought valiantly, and they were overcome. They were then stamped under foot. Probably it is physically impossible for our people, living softly and at ease, to visualize to themselves the dreadful woe that has come upon the people of Belgium, and especially upon the poor people. Let each man think of his neighbors – of the carpenter, the station agent, the day-laborer, the farmer, the grocer – who are round about him, and think of these men deprived of their all, their homes destroyed, their sons dead or prisoners, their wives and children half starved, overcome with fatigue and horror, stumbling their way to some city of refuge, and when they have reached it, finding air-ships wrecking the houses with bombs and destroying women and children. The King shared the toil and danger of the fighting men; the Queen and her children suffered as other mothers and children suffered.

Unquestionably what has been done in Belgium has been done in accordance with what the Germans sincerely believe to be the course of conduct necessitated by Germany's struggle for life. But Germany's need to struggle for her life does not make it any easier for the Belgians to suffer death. The Germans are in Belgium from no fault of the Belgians but purely because the Germans deemed it to their vital interest to violate Belgium's rights. Therefore the ultimate responsibility for what has occurred at Louvain and what has occurred and is occurring in Brussels rests upon Germany and in no way upon Belgium. The invasion could have been averted by no action of Belgium that was consistent with her honor and self-respect. The Belgians would have been less than men had they not defended themselves and their country. For this, and for this only, they are suffering, somewhat as my own German ancestors suffered when Turenne ravaged the Palatinate, somewhat as my Irish ancestors suffered in the struggles that attended the conquests and reconquests of Ireland in the days of Cromwell and William. The suffering is by no means as great, but it is very great, and it is altogether too nearly akin to what occurred in the seventeenth century for us of the twentieth century to feel overmuch pleased with the amount of advance that has been made. It is neither necessary nor at the present time possible to sift from the charges, countercharges, and denials the exact facts as to the acts alleged to have been committed in various places. The prime fact as regards Belgium is that Belgium was an entirely peaceful and genuinely neutral power which had been guilty of no offence whatever. What has befallen her is due to the further fact that a great, highly civilized military power deemed that its own vital interests rendered imperative the infliction of this suffering on an inoffensive although valiant and patriotic little nation.

I admire and respect the German people. I am proud of the German blood in my veins. But the sympathy and support of the American people should go out unreservedly to Belgium, and we should learn the lesson taught by Belgium's fall. What has occurred to Belgium is precisely what would occur under similar conditions to us, unless we were able to show that the action would be dangerous.

The rights and wrongs of these cases where nations violate the rules of morality in order to meet their own supposed needs can be precisely determined only when all the facts are known and when men's blood is cool. Nevertheless, it is imperative, in the interest of civilization, to create international conditions which shall neither require nor permit such action in the future. Moreover, we should understand clearly just what these actions are and just what lessons we of the United States should learn from them so far as our own future is concerned.

There are several such lessons. One is how complicated instead of how simple it is to decide what course we ought to follow as regards any given action supposed to be in the interest of peace. Of course I am speaking of the thing and not the name when I speak of peace. The ultrapacificists are capable of taking any position, yet I suppose that few among them now hold that there was value in the "peace" which was obtained by the concert of European powers when they prevented interference with Turkey while the Turks butchered some hundreds of thousands of Armenian men, women, and children. In the same way I do not suppose that even the ultrapacificists really feel that "peace" is triumphant in Belgium at the present moment. President Wilson has been much applauded by all the professional pacificists because he has announced that our desire for peace must make us secure it for ourselves by a neutrality so strict as to forbid our even whispering a protest against wrong-doing, lest such whispers might cause disturbance to our ease and well-being. We pay the penalty of this action – or, rather, supine inaction – on behalf of peace for ourselves, by forfeiting our right to do anything on behalf of peace for the Belgians in the present. We can maintain our neutrality only by refusal to do anything to aid unoffending weak powers which are dragged into the gulf of bloodshed and misery through no fault of their own. It is a grim comment on the professional pacificist theories as hitherto developed that, according to their view, our duty to preserve peace for ourselves necessarily means the abandonment of all effective effort to secure peace for other unoffending nations which through no fault of their own are trampled down by war.

The next lesson we should learn is of far more immediate consequence to us than speculations about peace in the abstract. Our people should wake up to the fact that it is a poor thing to live in a fool's paradise. What has occurred in this war ought to bring home to everybody what has of course long been known to all really well-informed men who were willing to face the truth and not try to dodge it. Until some method is devised of putting effective force behind arbitration and neutrality treaties neither these treaties nor the vague and elastic body of custom which is misleadingly termed international law will have any real effect in any serious crisis between us and any save perhaps one or two of the great powers. The average great military power looks at these matters purely from the standpoint of its own interests. Several months ago, for instance, Japan declared war on Germany. She has paid scrupulous regard to our own rights and feelings in the matter. The contention that she is acting in a spirit of mere disinterested altruism need not be considered. She believes that she has wrongs to redress and strong national interests to preserve. Nineteen years ago Germany joined with Russia to check Japan's progress after her victorious war with China, and has since then itself built up a German colonial possession on Chinese soil. Doubtless the Japanese have never for one moment forgotten this act of Germany. Doubtless they also regard the presence of a strong European military power in China so near to Korea and Manchuria as a menace to Japan's national life. With businesslike coolness the soldierly statesmen of Nippon have taken the chance which offered itself of at little cost retaliating for the injury inflicted upon them in the past and removing an obstacle to their future dominance in eastern Asia. Korea is absolutely Japan's. To be sure, by treaty it was solemnly covenanted that Korea should remain independent. But Korea was itself helpless to enforce the treaty, and it was out of the question to suppose that any other nation with no interest of its own at stake would attempt to do for the Koreans what they were utterly unable to do for themselves. Moreover, the treaty rested on the false assumption that Korea could govern herself well. It had already been shown that she could not in any real sense govern herself at all. Japan could not afford to see Korea in the hands of a great foreign power. She regarded her duty to her children and her children's children as overriding her treaty obligations. Therefore, when Japan thought the right time had come, it calmly tore up the treaty and took Korea, with the polite and businesslike efficiency it had already shown in dealing with Russia, and was afterward to show in dealing with Germany. The treaty, when tested, proved as utterly worthless as our own recent all-inclusive arbitration treaties – and worthlessness can go no further.

Hysteria does not tend toward edification; and in this country hysteria is unfortunately too often the earmark of the ultrapacificist. Surely at this time there is more reason than ever to remember Professor Lounsbury's remark concerning the "infinite capacity of the human brain to withstand the introduction of knowledge." The comments of some doubtless well-meaning citizens of our own country upon the lessons taught by this terrible cataclysm of war are really inexplicable to any man who forgets the truth that Professor Lounsbury thus set forth. A writer of articles for a newspaper syndicate the other day stated that Germany was being opposed by the rest of the world because it had "inspired fear." This thesis can, of course, be sustained. But Belgium has inspired no fear. Yet it has suffered infinitely more than Germany. Luxembourg inspired no fear. Yet it has been quietly taken possession of by Germany. The writer in question would find it puzzling to point out the particulars in which Belgium and Luxembourg – not to speak of China and Korea – are at this moment better off than Germany. Of course they are worse off; and this because Germany *has* "inspired fear," and they have not. Nevertheless, this writer drew the conclusion that "fear" was the only emotion which ought not to be inspired; and he advocated our abandonment of battle-ships and other means of defense, so that we might never inspire "fear" in any one. He forgot that, while it is a bad thing to inspire fear, it is a much worse thing to inspire contempt. Another newspaper writer pointed out that on the frontier between us and Canada there were no forts, and yet peace obtained; and drew the conclusion that forts and armed forces were inimical to national safety. This worthy soul evidently did not know that Luxembourg had no forts or armed forces, and therefore succumbed without a protest of any kind. If he does not admire the heroism of the Belgians and prefer it to the tame submission of the Luxembourgers, then this writer is himself unfit to live as a free man in a free country. The crown of ineptitude, however, was reached by an editor who announced, in praising the recent all-inclusive peace treaties, that "had their like been in existence between some of the European nations two weeks ago, the world might have been spared the great war." It is rather hard to deal seriously with such a supposition. At this very moment the utter worthlessness, under great pressure, of even the rational treaties drawn to protect Belgium and Luxembourg has been shown. To suppose that under such conditions a bundle of bits of paper representing mere verbiage, with no guarantee, would count for anything whatever in a serious crisis is to show ourselves unfit to control the destinies of a great, just, and self-respecting people.

These writers wish us to abandon all means of defending ourselves. Some of them advocate our abandoning the building of an efficient fleet. Yet at this moment Great Britain owes it that she is not in worse plight than Belgium solely to the fact that with far-sighted wisdom her statesmen have maintained her navy at the highest point of efficiency. At this moment the Japanese are at war with the Germans, and hostilities have been taking place in what but twenty years ago was Chinese territory, and what by treaty is unquestionably Chinese territory to-day. China has protested against the Japanese violation of Chinese neutrality in their operations against the Germans, but no heed has been paid to the protest, for China cannot back the protest by the use of armed force. Moreover, as China is reported to have pointed out to Germany, the latter power had violated Chinese neutrality just as Japan had done.

Very possibly the writers above alluded to were sincere in their belief that they were, advocating what was patriotic and wise when they urged that the United States make itself utterly defenseless so as to avoid giving an excuse for aggression. Yet these writers ought to have known that during their own lifetime China has been utterly defenseless and yet has suffered from aggression after aggression. Large portions of its territory are now in the possession of Russia, of Japan, of Germany, of France, of England. The great war between Russia and Japan was fought on what was nominally Chinese territory. At present, because a few months ago Serbian assassins murdered the heir to the Austrian monarchy, Japan has fought Germany on Chinese territory. Luxembourg has been absolutely powerless and defenseless, has had no soldiers and no forts. It is off the map at this moment. Not only are none of the belligerents thinking about its rights, but no neutral is thinking about its rights, and this simply because Luxembourg could not defend itself. It is our duty to be patient with every kind of folly, but it is hard for a good American, for a man to whom his country is dear and who reveres the memories of Washington and Lincoln, to be entirely patient with the kind of folly that advocates reducing this country to the position of China and Luxembourg.

One of the main lessons to learn from this war is embodied in the homely proverb: "Speak softly and carry a big stick." Persistently only half of this proverb has been quoted in deriding the men who wish to safeguard our national interest and honor. Persistently the effort has been made to insist that those who advocate keeping our country able to defend its rights are merely adopting "the policy of the big stick." In reality, we lay equal emphasis on the fact that it is necessary to speak softly; in other words, that it is necessary to be respectful toward all people and scrupulously to refrain from wronging them, while at the same time keeping ourselves in condition to prevent wrong being done to us. If a nation does not in this sense speak softly, then sooner or later the policy of the big stick is certain to result in war. But what befell Luxembourg five months ago, what has befallen China again and again during the past quarter of a century, shows that no amount of speaking softly will save any people which does not carry a big stick.

America should have a coherent policy of action toward foreign powers, and this should primarily be based on the determination never to give offense when it can be avoided, always to treat other nations justly and courteously, and, as long as present conditions exist, to be prepared to defend our own rights ourselves. No other nation will defend them for us. No paper guarantee or treaty will be worth the paper on which it is written if it becomes to the interest of some other power to violate it, unless we have strength, and courage and ability to use that strength, back of the treaty. Every public man, every writer who speaks with wanton offensiveness of a foreign power or of a foreign people, whether he attacks England or France or Germany, whether he assails the Russians or the Japanese, is doing an injury to the whole American body politic. We have plenty of shortcomings at home to correct before we start out to criticise the shortcomings of others. Now and then it becomes imperatively necessary in the interests of humanity, or in our own vital interest, to act in a manner which will cause offense to some other power. This is a lamentable necessity; but when the necessity arises we must meet it and act as we are honorably bound to act, no matter what offense is given. We must always weigh well our duties in such a case, and consider the rights of others as well as our own rights, in the interest of the world at large. If after such consideration it is evident that we are bound to act along a certain line of policy, then it is mere weakness to refrain from doing so because offense is thereby given. But we must never act wantonly or brutally, or without regard to the essentials of genuine morality – a morality considering our interests as well as the interests of others, and considering the interests of future generations as well as of the present generation. We must so conduct ourselves that every big nation and every little nation that behaves itself shall never have to think of us with fear, and shall have confidence not only in our justice but in our courtesy. Submission to wrong-doing on our part would be mere weakness and would invite and insure disaster. We must not submit to wrong done to our honor or to our vital national interests. But we must be scrupulously careful always to speak with courtesy and self-restraint to others, always to act decently to others, and to give no nation any justification for believing that it has anything to fear from us as long as it behaves with decency and uprightness.

Above all, let us avoid the policy of peace with insult, the policy of unpreparedness to defend our rights, with inability to restrain our representatives from doing wrong to or publicly speaking ill of others. The worst policy for the United States is to combine the unbridled tongue with the unready hand.

We in this country have of course come lamentably short of our ideals. Nevertheless, in some ways our ideals have been high, and at times we have measurably realized them. From the beginning we have recognized what is taught in the words of Washington, and again in the great crisis of our national life in the words of Lincoln, that in the past free peoples have generally split and sunk on that great rock of difficulty caused by the fact that a government which recognizes the liberties of the people is not usually strong enough to preserve the liberties of the people against outside aggression. Washington and Lincoln believed that ours was a strong people and therefore fit for a strong government. They believed that it was only weak peoples that had to fear strong governments, and that to us it was given to combine freedom and efficiency. They belonged among that line of statesmen and public servants whose existence has been the negation of the theory that goodness is always associated with weakness, and that strength always finds its expression in violent wrong-doing. Edward the Confessor represented exactly the type which treats weakness and virtue as interchangeable terms. His reign was the prime cause of the conquest of England. Godoy, the Spanish statesman, a century ago, by the treaties he entered into and carried out, actually earned the title of "Prince of Peace" instead of merely lecturing about it; and the result of his peacefulness was the loss by Spain of the vast regions which she then held in our country west of the Mississippi, and finally the overthrow of the Spanish national government, the setting up in Madrid of a foreign king by a foreign conqueror, and a long-drawn and incredibly destructive war. To statesmen of this kind Washington and Lincoln stand in as sharp contrast as they stand on the other side to the great absolutist chiefs such as Caesar, Napoleon, Frederick the Great, and Cromwell. What was true of the personality of Washington and Lincoln was true of the policy they sought to impress upon our nation. They were just as hostile to the theory that virtue was to be confounded with weakness as to the theory that strength justified wrong-doing. No abundance of the milder virtues will save a nation that has lost the virile qualities; and, on the other hand, no admiration of strength must make us deviate from the laws of righteousness. The kind of "peace" advocated by the ultrapacificists of 1776 would have meant that we never would have had a country; the kind of "peace" advocated by the ultrapacificists in the early '60's would have meant the absolute destruction of the country. It would have been criminal weakness for Washington not to have fought for the independence of this country, and for Lincoln not to have fought for the preservation of the Union; just as in an infinitely smaller degree it would have been criminal weakness for us if we had permitted wrong-doing in Cuba to go on forever unchecked, or if we had failed to insist on the building of the Panama Canal in exactly the fashion that we did insist; and, above all, if we had failed to build up our navy as during the last twenty years it has been built up. No alliance, no treaty, and no easy good-will of other nations will save us if we are not true to ourselves; and, on the other hand, if we wantonly give offense to others, if we excite hatred and fear, then some day we will pay a heavy penalty.

The most important lesson, therefore, for us to learn from Belgium's fate is that, as things in the world now are, we must in any great crisis trust for our national safety to our ability and willingness to defend ourselves by our own trained strength and courage. We must not wrong others; and for our own safety we must trust, not to worthless bits of paper unbacked by power, and to treaties that are fundamentally foolish, but to our own manliness and clear-sighted willingness to face facts.

There is, however, another lesson which this huge conflict may at least possibly teach. There is at least a chance that from this calamity a movement may come which will at once supplement and in the future perhaps altogether supplant the need of the kind of action so plainly indicated by the demands of the present. It is at least possible that the conflict will result in a growth of democracy in Europe, in at least a partial substitution of the rule of the people for the rule of those who esteem it their God-given right to govern the people. This, in its turn, would render it probably a little more unlikely that there would be a repetition of such disastrous warfare. I do not think that at present it would prevent the possibility of warfare. I think that in the great countries engaged, the peoples as a whole have been behind their sovereigns on both sides of this contest. Certainly the action of the Socialists in Germany, France, and Belgium, and, so far as we know, of the popular leaders in Russia, would tend to bear out the truth of this statement. But the growth of the power of the people, while it would not prevent war, would at least render it more possible than at present to make appeals which might result in some cases in coming to an accommodation based upon justice; for justice is what popular rule must be permanently based upon and must permanently seek to obtain or it will not itself be permanent.

Moreover, the horror that right-thinking citizens feel over the awful tragedies of this war can hardly fail to make sensible men take an interest in genuine peace movements and try to shape them so that they shall be more practical than at present. I most earnestly believe in every rational movement for peace. My objection is only to movements that do not in very fact tell in favor of peace or else that sacrifice righteousness to peace. Of course this includes objection to all treaties that make believe to do what, as a matter of fact, they fail to do. Under existing conditions universal and all-inclusive arbitration treaties have been utterly worthless, because where there is no power to compel nations to arbitrate, and where it is perfectly certain that some nations will pay no respect to such agreements unless they can be forced to do so, it is mere folly for others to trust to promises impossible of performance; and it is an act of positive bad faith to make these promises when it is certain that the nation making them would violate them. But this does not in the least mean that we must abandon hope of taking action which will lessen the chance of war and make it more possible to circumscribe the limits of war's devastation.

For this result we must largely trust to sheer growth in morality and intelligence among the nations themselves. For a hundred years peace has obtained between us and Great Britain. No frontier in Europe is as long as the frontier between Canada and ourselves, and yet there is not a fort, nor an armed force worthy of being called such, upon it. This does not result from any arbitration treaty or any other treaty. Such treaties as those now existing are as a rule observed only when they serve to make a record of conditions that already exist and which they do not create. The fact simply is that there has been such growth of good feeling and intelligence that war between us and the British Empire is literally an impossibility, and there is no more chance of military movements across the Canadian border than there is of such movement between New York and New Hampshire or Quebec and Ontario. Slowly but surely, I believe, such feelings will grow, until war between the Englishman and the German, or the Russian, or the Frenchman, or between any of them and the American, will be as unthinkable as now between the Englishman or Canadian and the American.

But something can be done to hasten this day by wise action. It may not be possible at once to have this action as drastic as would be ultimately necessary; but we should keep our purpose in view. The utter weakness of the Hague court, and the worthlessness when strain is put upon them of most treaties, spring from the fact that at present there is no means of enforcing the carrying out of the treaty or enforcing the decision of the court. Under such circumstances recommendations for universal disarmament stand on an intellectual par with recommendations to establish "peace" in New York City by doing away with the police. Disarmament of the free and liberty-loving nations would merely mean insuring the triumph of some barbarism or despotism, and if logically applied would mean the extinction of liberty and of all that makes civilization worth having throughout the world. But in view of what has occurred in this war, surely the time ought to be ripe for the nations to consider a great world agreement among all the civilized military powers *to back righteousness by force.* Such an agreement would establish an efficient world league for the peace of righteousness.

Chapter III

Unwise Peace Treaties a Menace to Righteousness

In studying certain lessons which should be taught the United States by this terrible world war, it is not necessary for us to try exactly to assess or apportion the blame. There are plenty of previous instances of violation of treaties to be credited to almost all the nations engaged on one side or the other. We need not try to puzzle out why Italy and Japan seemingly construed similar treaties of alliance in diametrically opposite ways; nor need we decide which was justified or whether both were justified. It is quite immaterial to us, as regards certain of the lessons taught, whether the treaties alleged to be violated affect Luxembourg on the one hand or Bosnia on the other, whether it is the neutrality of China or the neutrality of Belgium that is violated.

Yet again, we need always to keep in mind that, although it is culpable to break a treaty, it may be even worse recklessly to make a treaty which cannot be kept. Recklessness in making promises is the surest way in which to secure the discredit attaching to the breaking of promises. A treaty at present usually represents merely promise, not performance; and it is wicked to promise what will not or cannot be performed. Genuine good can even now be accomplished by narrowly limited and defined arbitration treaties which are not all-inclusive, if they deal with subjects on which arbitration can be accepted. This nation has repeatedly acted in obedience to such treaties; and great good has come from arbitrations in such cases as, for example, the Dogger Bank incident, when the Russian fleet fired on British trawlers during the Russo-Japanese war. But no good whatever has come from treaties that represented a sham; and under existing conditions it is hypocritical for a nation to announce that it will arbitrate questions of honor or vital interest, and folly to think that opponents will abide by such treaties. Bad although it is to negotiate such a treaty, it would be worse to abide by it.

Under these conditions it is mischievous to a degree for a nation to trust to any treaty of the type now existing to protect it in great crises. Take the case of China as a living and present-day example. China has shown herself utterly impotent to defend her neutrality. Again and again she made this evident in the past. Order was not well kept at home and above all she was powerless to defend herself from outside attack. She has not prepared for war. She has kept utterly unprepared for war. Yet she has suffered more from war, in our own time, than any military power in the world during the same period. She has fulfilled exactly the conditions advocated by these well-meaning persons who for the last five months have been saying in speeches, editorials, articles for syndicates, and the like that the United States ought not to keep up battle-ships and ought not to trust to fortifications nor in any way to be ready or prepared to defend herself against hostile attack, but should endeavor to secure peace by being so inoffensive and helpless as not to arouse fear in others. The well-meaning people who write these editorials and make these speeches ought to understand that though it is a bad thing for a nation to arouse fear it is an infinitely worse thing to excite contempt; and every editor or writer or public man who tells us that we ought not to have battle-ships and that we ought to trust entirely to well-intentioned foolish all-inclusive arbitration treaties and abandon fortifications and not keep prepared, is merely doing his best to bring contempt upon the United States and to insure disaster in the future.

Nor is China the only case in point. Luxembourg is a case in point. Korea is a case in point. Korea was utterly inoffensive and helpless. It neither took nor was capable of taking the smallest aggressive action against any one. It had no forts, no war-ships, no army worthy of the name. It excited no fear and no anger. But it did excite measureless contempt, and therefore it invited aggression.

The point I wish to make is, first, the extreme unwisdom and impropriety of making promises that cannot be kept, and, second, the utter futility of expecting that in any save exceptional cases a strong power will keep a promise which it finds to its disadvantage, unless there is some way of putting force back of the demand that the treaty be observed.

35

America has no claim whatever to superior virtue in this matter. We have shown an appalling recklessness in making treaties, especially all-inclusive arbitration treaties and the like, which in time of stress would not and could not be observed. When such a treaty is not observed the blame really rests upon the unwise persons who made the treaty. Unfortunately, however, this apportionment of blame cannot be made by outsiders. All they can say is that the country concerned – and I speak of the United States – does not keep faith. The responsibility for breaking an improper promise really rests with those who make it; but the penalty is paid by the whole country.

There are certain respects in which I think the United States can fairly claim to stand ahead of most nations in its regard for international morality. For example, last spring when we took Vera Cruz, there were individuals within the city who fired at our troops in exactly the same fashion as that which is alleged to have taken place in Louvain. But it never for one moment entered the heads of our people to destroy Vera Cruz. In the same way, when we promised freedom to Cuba, we kept our promise, and after establishing an orderly government in Cuba withdrew our army and left her as an independent power; performing an act which, as far as I know, is entirely without parallel in the dealings of stronger with weaker nations.

In the same way our action in San Domingo, when we took and administered her customs houses, represented a substantial and efficient achievement in the cause of international peace which stands high in the very honorable but scanty list of such actions by great nations in dealing with their less fortunate sisters. In the same way our handling of the Panama situation, both in the acquisition of the canal, in its construction, and in the attitude we have taken toward the dwellers on the Isthmus and all the nations of mankind, has been such as to reflect signal honor on our people. In the same way we returned the Chinese indemnity, because we deemed it excessive, just as previously we had returned a money indemnity to Japan. Similarly the disinterestedness with which we have administered the Philippines for the good of the Philippine people is something upon which we have a right to pride ourselves and shows the harm that would have been done had we not taken possession of the Philippines.

But, unfortunately, in dealing with schemes of universal peace and arbitration, we have often shown an unwillingness to fulfil proper promises which we had already made by treaty, coupled with a reckless willingness to make new treaties with all kinds of promises which were either improper and ought not to be kept or which, even if proper, could not and would not be kept. It has again and again proved exceedingly difficult to get Congress to appropriate money to pay some obligation which under treaty or arbitration or the like has been declared to be owing by us to the citizens of some foreign nation. Often we have announced our intention to make sweeping arbitration treaties or agreements at the very time when by our conduct we were showing that in actual fact we had not the slightest intention of applying them with the sweeping universality we promised. In these cases we were usually, although not always, right in our refusal to apply the treaties, or rather the principles set forth in the treaties, to the concrete case at issue; but we were utterly wrong, we were, even although perhaps unintentionally, both insincere and hypocritical, when at the same time we made believe we intended that these principles would be universally applied. This was particularly true in connection with the universal arbitration treaties which our government unsuccessfully endeavored to negotiate some three years ago. Our government announced at that time that we intended to enter into universal arbitration treaties under which we would arbitrate everything, even including questions of honor and of vital national interest. At the very time that this announcement was made and the negotiation of the treaties begun, the government in case after case where specific performance of its pledges was demanded responded with a flat refusal to do the very thing it had announced its intention of doing.

Recently, there have been negotiated in Washington thirty or forty little all-inclusive arbitration or so-called "peace" treaties, which represent as high a degree of fatuity as is often achieved in these matters. There is no likelihood that they will do us any great material harm because it is absolutely certain that we would not pay the smallest attention to them in the event of their being invoked in any matter where our interests were seriously involved; but it would do us moral harm to break them, even although this were the least evil of two evil alternatives. It is a discreditable thing that at this very moment, with before our eyes such proof of the worthlessness of the neutrality treaties affecting Belgium and Luxembourg, our nation should be negotiating treaties which convince every sensible and well-informed observer abroad that we are either utterly heedless in making promises which cannot be kept or else willing to make promises which we have no intention of keeping. What has just happened shows that such treaties are worthless except to the degree that force can and will be used in backing them.

There are some well-meaning people, misled by mere words, who doubtless think that treaties of this kind do accomplish something. These good and well-meaning people may feel that I am not zealous in the cause of peace. This is the direct reverse of the truth. I abhor war. In common with all other thinking men I am inexpressibly saddened by the dreadful contest now waging in Europe. I put peace very high as an agent for bringing about righteousness. But if I must choose between righteousness and peace I choose righteousness. Therefore, I hold myself in honor bound to do anything in my power to advance the cause of the peace of righteousness throughout the world. I believe we can make substantial advances by international agreement in the line of achieving this purpose and in this book I state in outline just what I think can be done toward this end. But I hold that we will do nothing and less than nothing unless, pending the accomplishment of this purpose, we keep our own beloved country in such shape that war shall not strike her down; and, furthermore, unless we also seriously consider what the defects have been in the existing peace, neutrality, and arbitration treaties and in the attitude hitherto assumed by the professional pacificists, which have rendered these treaties such feeble aids to peace and the ultrapacificist attitude a positive obstacle to peace.

The truth is that the advocates of world-wide peace, like all reformers, should bear in mind Josh Billings's astute remark that "it is much easier to be a harmless dove than a wise serpent." The worthy pacificists have completely forgotten that the Biblical injunction is two-sided and that we are bidden not only to be harmless as doves but also to be wise as serpents. The ultrapacificists have undoubtedly been an exceedingly harmless body so far as obtaining peace is concerned. They have exerted practically no influence in restraining wrong, although they have sometimes had a real and lamentable influence in crippling the forces of right and preventing them from dealing with wrong. An appreciable amount of good work has been done for peace by genuine lovers of peace, but it has not been done by the feeble folk of the peace movement, loquacious but impotent, who are usually unfortunately prominent in the movement and who excite the utter derision of the great powers of evil.

Sincere lovers of peace who are wise have been obliged to face the fact that it is often a very complicated thing to secure peace without the sacrifice of righteousness. Furthermore, they have been obliged to face the fact that generally the only way to accomplish anything was by not trying to accomplish too much.

The complicated nature of the problem is shown by the fact that whereas the real friends of righteousness believe that our duty to peace ought to be fulfilled by protesting against – and doubtless if necessary doing more than merely protest against – the violation of the rights secured to Belgium by treaty, the professional pacificists nervously point out that such a course would expose us to accusations of abandoning our "neutrality." In theory these pacificists admit it to be our duty to uphold the Hague treaties of which we were among the signatory powers; but they are against effective action to uphold them, for they are pathetic believers in the all-sufficiency of signatures, placed on bits of paper. They have pinned their faith to the foolish belief that everything put in these treaties was forthwith guaranteed to all mankind. In dealing with the rights of neutrals Article 10 of Chapter 1 explicitly states that if the territory of a neutral nation is invaded the repelling of such invasion by force shall not be esteemed a "hostile" act on the part of the neutral nation. Unquestionably under this clause Belgium has committed no hostile act. Yet, this sound declaration of morality, in a treaty that the leading world-powers have signed, amounts to precisely and exactly nothing so far as the rights of poor Belgium are concerned, because there is no way provided of enforcing the treaty and because the American government has decided that it can keep at peace and remain neutral only by declining to do what, according to the intention of the Hague treaty, it would be expected to do in securing peace for

Belgium. In practice the Hague treaties have proved and will always prove useless while there is no sanction of force behind them. For the United States to proffer "good offices" to the various powers entering such a great conflict as the present one accomplishes not one particle of good; to refer them, when they mutually complain of wrongs, to a Hague court which is merely a phantom does less than no good. The Hague treaties can accomplish nothing, and ought not to have been entered into, unless in such a case as this of Belgium there is willingness to take efficient action under them. There could be no better illustration of how extremely complicated and difficult a thing it is in practice instead of in theory to make even a small advance in the cause of peace.

I believe that international opinion can do something to arrest wrong; but only if it is aroused and finds some method of clear and forceful expression. For example, I hope that it has been aroused to the point of preventing any repetition at the expense of Brussels of the destruction which has befallen Louvain. The peaceful people of Brussels now live in dread of what may happen to them if the Germans should evacuate the city. In such an event it is possible that half a dozen fanatics, or half a dozen young roughs of the "Apache" type, in spite of everything that good citizens may do, will from some building fire on the retiring soldiers. In such case the offenders ought to be and must be treated with instant and unsparing rigor, and those clearly guilty of aiding or shielding them should also be so treated. But if in such case Brussels is in whole or in part destroyed as Louvain was destroyed, those destroying it will be guilty of a capital crime against civilization; and it is heartily to be regretted that civilized nations have not devised some method by which the collective power of civilization can be used to prevent or punish such crimes. In every great city there are plenty of reckless or fanatical or downright evil men eagerly ready to do some act which is abhorrent to the vast majority of their fellows; and it is wicked to punish with cruel severity immense multitudes of innocent men, women, and children for the misdeeds of a few rascals or fanatics. Of course, it is eminently right to punish by death these rascals or fanatics themselves.

Kindly people who know little of life and nothing whatever of the great forces of international rivalry have exposed the cause of peace

40

to ridicule by believing that serious wars could be avoided through arbitration treaties, peace treaties, neutrality treaties, and the action of the Hague court, without putting force behind such treaties and such action. The simple fact is that none of these existing treaties and no function of the Hague court hitherto planned and exercised have exerted or could exert the very smallest influence in maintaining peace when great conflicting international passions are aroused and great conflicting national interests are at stake. It happens that wars have been more numerous in the fifteen years since the first Hague conference than in the fifteen years prior to it. It was Russia that called the first and second Hague conferences, and in the interval she fought the war with Japan and is now fighting a far greater war. We bore a prominent part at the Hague conferences; but if the Hague court had been in existence in 1898 it could not have had the smallest effect upon our war with Spain; and neither would any possible arbitration treaty or peace treaty have had any effect. At the present moment Great Britain owes its immunity from invasion purely to its navy and to the fact that that navy has been sedulously exercised in time of peace so as to prepare it for war. Great Britain has always been willing to enter into any reasonable – and into some unreasonable – peace and arbitration treaties; but her fate now would have been the fate of Belgium and would not have been hindered in the smallest degree by these treaties, if she had not possessed a first-class navy. The navy has done a thousand times more for her peace than all the arbitration treaties and peace treaties of the type now existing that the wit of man could invent. I believe that national agreement in the future can do much toward minimizing the chance for war; but it must be by proceeding along different lines from those hitherto followed and in an entirely different spirit from the ultrapacificist or professional peace-at-any-price spirit.

The Hague court has served a very limited, but a useful, purpose. Some, although only a small number, of the existing peace and arbitration treaties have served a useful purpose. But the purpose and the service have been strictly limited. Issues often arise between nations which are not of first-class importance, which do not affect their vital honor and interest, but which, if left unsettled, may eventually cause irritation that will have the worst possible results. The Hague court and the different treaties in question provide instrumentalities for settling such disputes, where the nations involved really wish to settle them but might be unable to do so if means were not supplied. This is a real service and one well worth rendering. These treaties and the Hague court have rendered such service again and again in time past. It has been a misfortune that some worthy people have anticipated too much and claimed too much in reference to them, for the failure of the excessive claims has blinded men to what they really have accomplished. To expect from them what they cannot give is merely shortsighted. To assert that they will give what they cannot give is mischievous. To promise that they will give what they cannot give is not only mischievous but hypocritical; and it is for this reason that such treaties as the thirty or forty all-inclusive arbitration or peace treaties recently negotiated at Washington, although unimportant, are slightly harmful.

The Hague court has proved worthless in the present gigantic crisis. There is hardly a Hague treaty which in the present crisis has not in some respect been violated. However, a step toward the peaceful settlement of questions at issue between nations which are not vital and which do not mark a serious crisis has been accomplished on certain occasions in the past by the action of the Hague court and by rational and limited peace or arbitration treaties. Our business is to try to make this court of more effect and to enlarge the class of cases where its actions will be valuable. In order to do this, we must endeavor to put an international police force behind this international judiciary. At the same time we must refuse to do or say anything insincere. Above all, we must refuse to be misled into abandoning the policy of efficient self-defense, by any unfounded trust that the Hague court, as now constituted, and peace or arbitration treaties of the existing type, can in the smallest degree accomplish what they never have accomplished and never can accomplish. Neither the existing Hague court nor any peace treaties of the existing type will exert even the slightest influence in saving from disaster any nation that does not preserve the virile virtues and the long-sightedness that will enable it by its own might to guard its own honor, interest, and national life.

Chapter IV

The Causes of the War

From what we have so far considered, two things are evident. First, it is quite clear that in the world, as it is at this moment situated, it is literally criminal, literally a crime against the nation, not to be adequately and thoroughly prepared in advance, so as to guard ourselves and hold our own in war. We should have a much better army than at present, including especially a far larger reserve upon which to draw in time of war. We should have first-class fortifications, especially on the canal and in Hawaii. Most important of all, we should not only have a good navy but should have it continually exercised in manœuvring. For nearly two years our navy has totally lacked the practice in manœuvring in fleet formation indispensable to its efficiency.

Of all the lessons hitherto taught by the war, the most essential for us to take to heart is that taught by the catastrophe that has befallen Belgium. One side of this catastrophe, one lesson taught by Belgium's case, is the immense gain in the self-respect of a people that has dared to fight heroically in the face of certain disaster and possible defeat. Every Belgian throughout the world carries his head higher now than he has ever carried it before, because of the proof of virile strength that his people have given. In the world at large there is not the slightest interest concerning Luxembourg's ultimate fate; there is nothing more than amusement as to the discussion whether Japan or Germany is most to blame in connection with the infringement of Chinese neutrality. This is because neither China nor Luxembourg has been able and willing effectively to stand for her own rights. At this moment Luxembourg is enjoying "peace" – the peace of death. But Belgium has stood for her own rights. She has shown heroism, courage, and self-sacrifice, and, great though the penalty, the ultimate reward will be greater still.

If ever this country is attacked and drawn into war as Belgium, through no fault of her own, was drawn into war, I hope most earnestly that she will emulate Belgium's courage; and this she cannot do unless she is prepared in advance as Belgium was prepared. In one point, as I have already stated, I very earnestly hope that she will go beyond Belgium. If any great city, such as New York or San Francisco, Boston or Seattle, is held for ransom by a foreign foe, I earnestly hope that Americans, within the city and without, will insist that not one dollar of ransom shall be paid, and will gladly acquiesce in the absolute destruction of the city, by fire or in any other manner, rather than see a dollar paid into the war chest of our foes for the further prosecution of the war against us. Napoleon the Great made many regions pay for their own conquest and the conquest of the nations to which they belonged. But Spain and Russia would not pay, and the burning of Moscow and the defense of Saragossa marked the two great stages in the turn of the tide against him. The prime lesson of this war is that no nation can preserve its own self-respect, or the good-will of other nations, unless it keeps itself ready to exact justice from others, precisely as it should keep itself eager and willing to do justice to others.

The second lesson is the utter inadequacy in times of great crises of existing peace and neutrality treaties, and of all treaties conceived in the spirit of the all-inclusive arbitration treaties recently adopted at Washington; and, in fact, of all treaties which do not put potential force behind the treaty, which do not create some kind of international police power to stand behind international sense of right as expressed in some competent tribunal.

It remains to consider whether there is not – and I believe there is – some method which will bring nearer the day when international war of the kind hitherto waged and now waging between nations shall be relegated to that past which contains the kind of private war that was habitually waged between individuals up to the end of the Middle Ages. By degrees the work of a national police has been substituted for the exercise of the right of private war. The growth of sentiment in favor of peace within each nation accomplished little until an effective police force was put back of the sentiment. There are a few communities where such a police force is almost nonexistent, although always latent in the shape of a sheriff's posse or something of the kind. In all big communities, however, in all big cities, law is observed, innocent and law-abiding and peaceful people are protected and the disorderly and violent classes prevented from a riot of mischief and wrong-doing only by the presence of an efficient police force. Some analogous international police force must be created if war between nations is to be minimized as war between individuals has been minimized.

It is, of course, essential that, if this end is to be accomplished, we shall face facts with the understanding of what they really signify. Not the slightest good is done by hysterical outcries for a peace which would consecrate wrong or leave wrongs unredressed. Little or nothing would be gained by a peace which merely stopped this war for the moment and left untouched all the causes that have brought it about. A peace which left the wrongs of Belgium unredressed, which did not leave her independent and secured against further wrong-doing, and which did not provide measures hereafter to safeguard all peaceful nations against suffering the fate that Belgium has suffered, would be mischievous rather than beneficial in its ultimate effects. If the United States had any part in bringing about such a peace it would be deeply to our discredit as a nation. Belgium has been terribly wronged, and the civilized world owes it to itself to see that this wrong is redressed and that steps are taken which will guarantee that hereafter conditions shall not be permitted to become such as either to require or to permit such action as that of Germany against Belgium. Surely all good and honest men who are lovers of peace and who do not use the great words "love of peace" to cloak their own folly and timidity must agree that peace is to be made the handmaiden of righteousness or else that it is worthless.

England's attitude in going to war in defense of Belgium's rights, according to its guarantee, was not only strictly proper but represents the only kind of action that ever will make a neutrality treaty or peace treaty or arbitration treaty worth the paper on which it is written. The published despatches of the British government show that Sir Edward Grey clearly, emphatically, and scrupulously declined to commit his government to war until it became imperative to do so if Great Britain was to fulfil, as her honor and interest alike demanded, her engagements on behalf of the neutrality of Belgium. Of course, as far as Great Britain is concerned, she would not be honorably justified in making peace unless this object of her going to war was achieved. Our hearty sympathy should go out to her in this attitude.

The case of Belgium in this war stands by itself. As regards all the other powers, it is not only possible to make out a real case in favor of every nation on each side, but it is also quite possible to show that, under existing conditions, each nation was driven by its vital interests to do what it did. The real nature of the problem we have ahead of us can only be grasped if this attitude of the several powers is thoroughly understood. To paint the Kaiser as a devil, merely bent on gratifying a wicked thirst for bloodshed, is an absurdity, and worse than an absurdity. I believe that history will declare that the Kaiser acted in conformity with the feelings of the German people and as he sincerely believed the interests of his people demanded; and, as so often before in his personal and family life, he and his family have given honorable proof that they possess the qualities that are characteristic of the German people. Every one of his sons went to the war, not nominally, but to face every danger and hardship. Two of his sons hastily married the girls to whom they were betrothed and immediately afterward left for the front.

This was a fresh illustration of one of the most striking features of the outbreak of the war in Germany. In tens of thousands of cases the officers and enlisted men, who were engaged, married immediately before starting for the front. In many of the churches there were long queues of brides waiting for the ceremony, so as to enable their lovers to marry them just before they responded to the order that meant that they might have to sacrifice everything, including life, for the nation. A nation that shows such a spirit is assuredly a great nation. The efficiency of the German organization, the results of the German preparation in advance, were strikingly shown in the powerful forward movement of the first six weeks of the war and in the steady endurance and resolute resourcefulness displayed in the following months.

Not only is the German organization, the German preparedness, highly creditable to Germany, but even more creditable is the spirit lying behind the organization. The men and women of Germany, from the highest to the lowest, have shown a splendid patriotism and abnegation of self. In reading of their attitude, it is impossible not to feel a thrill of admiration for the stern courage and lofty disinterestedness which this great crisis laid bare in the souls of the people. I most earnestly hope that we Americans, if ever the need may arise, will show similar qualities.

It is idle to say that this is not a people's war. The intensity of conviction in the righteousness of their several causes shown by the several peoples is a prime factor for consideration, if we are to take efficient means to try to prevent a repetition of this incredible world tragedy. History may decide in any war that one or the other party was wrong, and yet also decide that the highest qualities and powers of the human soul were shown by that party. We here in the United States have now grown practically to accept this view as regards our own Civil War, and we feel an equal pride in the high devotion to the right, as it was given each man to see the right, shown alike by the men who wore the blue and the men who wore the gray.

The English feel that in this war they fight not only for themselves but for principle, for justice, for civilization, for a real and lasting world peace. Great Britain is backed by the great free democracies that under her flag have grown up in Canada, in Australia, in South Africa. She feels that she stands for the liberties and rights of weak nations everywhere. One of the most striking features of the war is the way in which the varied peoples of India have sprung to arms to defend the British Empire.

The Russians regard the welfare of their whole people as at stake. The Russian Liberals believe that success for Russia means an end of militarism in Europe. They believe that the Pole, the Jew, the Finn, the man of the Caucasus will each and all be enfranchised, that the advance of justice and right in Russia will be immeasurably furthered by the triumph of the Russian people in this contest, and that the conflict was essential, not only to Russian national life but to the growth of freedom and justice within her boundaries.

The people of Germany believe that they are engaged primarily in a fight for life of the Teuton against the Slav, of civilization against what they regard as a vast menacing flood of barbarism. They went to war because they believed the war was an absolute necessity, not merely to German well-being but to German national existence. They sincerely feel that the nations of western Europe are traitors to the cause of Occidental civilization, and that they themselves are fighting, each man for his own hearthstone, for his own wife and children, and all for the future existence of the generations yet to come.

The French feel with passionate conviction that this is the last stand of France, and that if she does not now succeed and is again trampled under foot, her people will lose for all time their place in the forefront of that great modern civilization of which the debt to France is literally incalculable. It would be impossible too highly to admire the way in which the men and women of France have borne themselves in this nerve-shattering time of awful struggle and awful suspense. They have risen level to the hour's need, whereas in 1870 they failed so to rise. The high valor of the French soldiers has been matched by the poise, the self-restraint, the dignity and the resolution with which the French people and the French government have behaved.

Of Austria and Hungary, of Serbia and Montenegro, exactly the same is true, and the people of each of these countries have shown the sternest and most heroic courage and the loftiest and most patriotic willingness for self-sacrifice.

To each of these peoples the war seems a crusade against threatening wrong, and each man fervently believes in the justice of his cause. Moreover, each combatant fights with that terrible determination to destroy the opponent which springs from fear. It is not the fear which any one of these powers has inspired that offers the difficult problem. It is the fear which each of them genuinely feels. Russia believes that a quarter of the Slav people will be trodden under the heel of the Germans, unless she succeeds. France and England believe that their very existence depends on the destruction of the German menace. Germany believes that unless she can so cripple, and, if possible, destroy her western foes, as to make them harmless in the future, she will be unable hereafter to protect herself against the mighty Slav people on her eastern boundary and will be reduced to a condition of international impotence. Some of her leaders are doubtless influenced by worse motives; but the motives above given are, I believe, those that influence the great mass of Germans, and these are in their essence merely the motives of patriotism, of devotion to one's people and one's native land.

We nations who are outside ought to recognize both the reality of this fear felt by each nation for others, together with the real justification for its existence. Yet we cannot sympathize with that fear-born anger which would vent itself in the annihilation of the conquered. The right attitude is to limit militarism, to destroy the menace of militarism, but to preserve the national integrity of each nation. The contestants are the great civilized peoples of Europe and Asia.

Japan's part in the war has been slight. She has borne herself with scrupulous regard not only to the rights but to the feelings of the people of the United States. Japan's progress should be welcomed by every enlightened friend of humanity because of the promise it contains for the regeneration of Asia. All that is necessary in order to remove every particle of apprehension caused by this progress is to do what ought to be done in reference to her no less than in reference to European and American powers, namely, to develop a world policy which shall guarantee each nation against any menace that might otherwise be held for it in the growth and progress of another nation.

The destruction of Russia is not thinkable, but if it were, it would be a most frightful calamity. The Slavs are a young people, of limitless possibilities, who from various causes have not been able to develop as rapidly as the peoples of central and western Europe. They have grown in civilization until their further advance has become something greatly to be desired, because it will be a factor of immense importance in the welfare of the world. All that is necessary is for Russia to throw aside the spirit of absolutism developed in her during the centuries of Mongol dominion. She will then be found doing what no other race can do and what it is of peculiar advantage to the English-speaking peoples that she should do.

As for crushing Germany or crippling her and reducing her to political impotence, such an action would be a disaster to mankind. The Germans are not merely brothers; they are largely ourselves. The debt we owe to German blood is great; the debt we owe to German thought and to German example, not only in governmental administration but

49

in all the practical work of life, is even greater. Every generous heart and every far-seeing mind throughout the world should rejoice in the existence of a stable, united, and powerful Germany, too strong to fear aggression and too just to be a source of fear to its neighbors.

As for France, she has occupied, in the modern world, a position as unique as Greece in the world of antiquity. To have her broken or cowed would mean a loss to-day as great as the loss that was suffered by the world when the creative genius of the Greek passed away with his loss of political power and material greatness. The world cannot spare France.

Now, the danger to each of these great and splendid civilizations arises far more from the fear that each feels than from the fear that each inspires. Belgium's case stands apart. She inspired no fear. No peace should be made until her wrongs have been redressed, and the likelihood of the repetition of such wrongs provided against. She has suffered incredibly because the fear among the plain German people, among the Socialists, for instance, of the combined strength of France and Russia made them acquiesce in and support the policy of the military party, which was to disregard the laws of international morality and the plain and simple rights of the Belgian people.

It is idle merely to make speeches and write essays against this fear, because at present the fear has a real basis. At present each nation has cause for the fear it feels. Each nation has cause to believe that its national life is in peril unless it is able to take the national life of one or more of its foes or at least hopelessly to cripple that foe. The causes of the fear must be removed or, no matter what peace may be patched up to-day or what new treaties may be negotiated to-morrow, these causes will at some future day bring about the same results, bring about a repetition of this same awful tragedy.

Chapter V

How to Strive for World Peace

In the preceding chapters I have endeavored to set forth, in a spirit of absolute fairness and calmness, the lessons as I see them that this war teaches all the world and especially the United States. I believe I have shown that, while, at least as against Belgium, there has been actual wrong-doing, yet on the whole and looking back at the real and ultimate causes rather than at the temporary occasions of the war, what has occurred is due primarily to the intense fear felt by each nation for other nations and to the anger born of that fear. Doubtless in certain elements, notably certain militaristic elements, of the population other motives have been at work; but I believe that the people of each country, in backing the government of that country, in the present war have been influenced mainly by a genuine patriotism and a genuine fear of what might happen to their beloved land in the event of aggression by other nations.

Under such conditions, as I have shown, our duty is twofold. In the first place, events have clearly demonstrated that in any serious crisis treaties unbacked by force are not worth the paper upon which they are written. Events have clearly shown that it is the idlest of folly to assert and little short of treason against the nation for statesmen who should know better to pretend, that the salvation of any nation under existing world conditions can be trusted to treaties, to little bits of paper with names signed on them but without any efficient force behind them. The United States will be guilty of criminal misconduct, we of this generation will show ourselves traitors to our children and our children's children if, as conditions are now, we do not keep ourselves ready to defend our hearths, trusting in great crises not to treaties, not to the ineffective good-will of outsiders, but to our own stout hearts and strong hands.

So much for the first and most vital lesson. But we are not to be excused if we stop here. We must endeavor earnestly but with sanity to try to bring around better world conditions. We must try to shape our policy in conjunction with other nations so as to bring nearer the day when the peace of righteousness, the peace of justice and fair dealing, will be established among the nations of the earth. With this object in view, it is our duty carefully to weigh the influences which are at work or may be put to work in order to bring about this result and in every effective way to do our best to further the growth of these influences. When this has been done no American administration will be able to assert that it is reduced to humiliating impotence even to protest against such wrong as that committed on Belgium, because, forsooth, our "neutrality" can only be preserved by failure to help right what is wrong – and we shall then as a people have too much self-respect to enter into absurd, all-inclusive arbitration treaties, unbacked by force, at the very moment when we fail to do what is clearly demanded by our duty under the Hague treaties.

Doubtless in the long run most is to be hoped from the slow growth of a better feeling, a more real feeling of brotherhood among the nations, among the peoples. The experience of the United States shows that there is no real foundation in race for the bitter antagonism felt among Slavs and Germans, French and English. There are in this country hundreds of thousands, millions, of men who by birth and parentage are of German descent, of French descent or Slavonic descent, or descended from each of the peoples within the British Islands. These different races not only get along well together here, but become knit into one people, and after a few generations their blood is mingled. In my own veins runs not only the blood of ancestors from the various peoples of the British Islands, English, Scotch, Welsh, and Irish, but also the blood of Frenchman and of German – not to speak of my forefathers from Holland. It is idle to tell us that the Frenchman and the German, the Slav and the Englishman are irreconcilably hostile one to the other because of difference of race. From our own daily experiences we know the contrary. We know that good men and bad men are to be found in each race. We know that the differences between the races above named and many others are infinitesimal compared with the vital points of likeness.

But this growth is too slow by itself adequately to meet present needs. At present we are confronted with the fact that each nation must keep armed and must be ready to go to war because there is a real and desperate need to do so and because the penalty for failure may be to suffer a fate like that of China. At present in every great crisis treaties have shown themselves not worth the paper they are written on, and the multitude of peace congresses that have been held have failed to secure even the slightest tangible result, as regards any contest in which the passions of great nations were fully aroused and their vital interests really concerned. In other words, each nation at present in any crisis of fundamental importance has to rely purely on its own power, its own strength, its own individual force. The futility of international agreements in great crises has come from the fact that force was not back of them.

What is needed in international matters is to create a judge and then to put police power back of the judge.

So far the time has not been ripe to attempt this. Surely now, in view of the awful cataclysm of the present war, such a plan could at least be considered; and it may be that the combatants at the end will be willing to try it in order to secure at least a chance for the only kind of peace that is worth having, the peace that is compatible with self-respect. Merely to bring about a peace at the present moment, without providing for the elimination of the causes of war, would accomplish nothing of any permanent value, and the attempt to make it would probably represent nothing else than the adroit use of some more or less foolish or more or less self-interested outsider by some astute power which wished to see if it could not put its opponents in the wrong.

If the powers were justified in going into this war by their vital interests, then they are required to continue the war until these vital interests are no longer in jeopardy. A peace which left without redress wrongs like those which Belgium has suffered or which in effect consecrated the partial or entire destruction of one or more nations and the survival in aggravated form of militarism and autocracy, and of international hatred in its most intense and virulent form, would really be only a worthless truce and would not represent the slightest advance in the cause of righteousness and of international morality.

The essential thing to do is to free each nation from the besetting fear of its neighbor. This can only be done by removing the causes of such fear. The neighbor must no longer be a danger.

Mere disarmament will not accomplish this result, and the disarmament of the free and enlightened peoples, so long as a single despotism or barbarism were left armed, would be a hideous calamity. If armaments were reduced while causes of trouble were in no way removed, wars would probably become somewhat more frequent just because they would be less expensive and less decisive. It is greatly to be desired that the growth of armaments should be arrested, but they cannot be arrested while present conditions continue. Mere treaties, mere bits of papers, with names signed to them and with no force back of them, have proved utterly worthless for the protection of nations, and where they are the only alternatives it is not only right but necessary that each nation should arm itself so as to be able to cope with any possible foe.

The one permanent move for obtaining peace, which has yet been suggested, with any reasonable chance of attaining its object, is by an agreement among the great powers, in which each should pledge itself not only to abide by the decisions of a common tribunal but to back with force the decisions of that common tribunal. The great civilized nations of the world which do possess force, actual or immediately potential, should combine by solemn agreement in a great World League for the Peace of Righteousness. In a later chapter I shall briefly outline what such an agreement should attempt to perform. At present it is enough to say that such a world-agreement offers the only alternative to each nation's relying purely on its own armed strength; for a treaty unbacked by force is in no proper sense of the word an alternative.

Of course, if there were not reasonable good faith among the nations making such an agreement, it would fail. But it would not fail merely because one nation did not observe good faith. It would be impossible to say that such an agreement would at once and permanently bring universal peace. But it would certainly mark an immense advance. It would certainly mean that the chances of war were minimized and the prospects of limiting and confining and regulating war immensely increased. At present force, as represented by the armed strength of the nations, is wholly divorced from such instrumentalities for securing peace as international agreements and treaties. In consequence, the latter are practically impotent in great crises. There is no connection between force, on the one hand, and any scheme for securing international peace or justice on the other. Under these conditions every wise and upright nation must continue to rely for its own peace and well-being on its own force, its own strength. As all students of the law know, a right without a remedy is in no real sense of the word a right at all. In international matters the declaration of a right, or the announcement of a worthy purpose, is not only aimless, but is a just cause for derision and may even be mischievous, if force is not put behind the right or the purpose. Our business is to make force the agent of justice, the instrument of right in international matters as it has been made in municipal matters, in matters within each nation.

One good purpose which would be served by the kind of international action I advocate is that of authoritatively deciding when treaties terminate or lapse. At present every treaty ought to contain provision for its abrogation; and at present the wrong done in disregarding a treaty may be one primarily of time and manner. Unquestionably it may become an imperative duty to abrogate a treaty. The Supreme Court of the United States set forth this right and duty in convincing manner when discussing our treaty with France during the administration of John Adams, and again a century later when discussing the Chinese treaty. The difficulty at present is that each case must be treated on its own merits; for in some cases it may be right and necessary for a nation to abrogate or denounce (not to violate) a treaty; and yet in other cases such abrogation may represent wrong-doing which should be suppressed by the armed strength of civilization. At present in cases where only two nations are concerned there is no substitute for such abrogation or violation of the treaty by one of them; for each of the two has to be judge in its own case. But the tribunal of a world league would offer the proper place to which to apply for the abrogation of treaties; and, with international force back of such a tribunal, the infraction of a treaty could be punished in whatever way the necessities of the case demanded.

Such a scheme as the one hereinafter briefly outlined will not bring perfect justice any more than under municipal law we obtain perfect justice; but it will mark an immeasurable advance on anything now existing; for it will mean that at last a long stride has been taken in the effort to put the collective strength of civilized mankind behind the collective purpose of mankind to secure the peace of righteousness, the peace of justice among the nations of the earth.

It may be, though I sincerely hope to the contrary, that such a scheme is for the immediate future Utopian – it certainly will not be Utopian for the remote future. If it is impossible in the immediate future to devise some working scheme by which force shall be put behind righteousness in disinterested and effective fashion, where international wrongs are concerned, then the only alternative will be for each free people to keep itself in shape with its own strength to defend its own rights and interests, and meanwhile to do all that can be done to help forward the slow growth of sentiment which is assuredly, although very gradually, telling against international wrong-doing and violence.

Man, in recognizedly human shape, has been for ages on this planet, and the extraordinary discoveries in Egypt and Mesopotamia now enable us to see in dim fashion the beginning of historic times six or seven thousand years ago. In the earlier ages of which history speaks there was practically no such thing as an international conscience. The armies of Babylon and Assyria, Egypt and Persia felt no sense of obligation to outsiders and conquered merely because they wished to conquer. In Greece a very imperfect recognition of international right grew up so far as Greek communities were concerned, but it never extended to barbarians. In the Roman Empire this feeling grew slightly, if only for the reason that so many nations were included within its bounds and were forced to live peaceably together. In the Middle Ages the common Christianity of Europe created a real bond. There was at least a great deal of talk about the duties of Christian nations to one another; and although the action along the lines of the talk was lamentably insufficient, still the talk itself represented the dawning recognition of the fact that each nation might owe something to other nations and that it was not right to base action purely on self-interest.

There has undoubtedly been a wide expansion of this feeling during the last few centuries, and particularly during the last century. It now extends so as to include not only Christian nations but also those non-Christian nations which themselves treat with justice and fairness the men of different creed. We are still a lamentably long distance away from the goal toward which we are striving; but we have taken a few steps toward that goal. A hundred years ago the English-speaking peoples of Britain and America regarded one another as inveterate and predestined enemies, just as three centuries previously had been the case in Great Britain itself between those who dwelt in the northern half and those who dwelt in the southern half of the island. Now war is unthinkable between us. Moreover, there is a real advance in goodwill, respect, and understanding between the United States and all the other nations of the earth. The advance is not steady and it is interrupted at times by acts of unwisdom, which are quite as apt to be committed by ourselves as by other peoples; but the advance has gone on. There is far greater sentiment than ever before against unwarranted aggressions by stronger powers against weak powers; there is far greater feeling against misconduct, whether in small or big powers; and far greater feeling against brutality in war.

This does not mean that the wrong-doing as regards any one of these matters has as yet been even approximately stopped or that the indignation against such wrong-doing is as yet anything like as effective as it should be. But we must not let our horror at the wrong that is still done blind us to the fact that there has been improvement. As late as the eighteenth century there were continual instances where small nations or provinces were overrun, just as Belgium has been overrun, without any feeling worth taking into account being thereby excited in the rest of mankind. In the seventeenth century affairs were worse. What has been done in Belgian cities has been very dreadful and the Belgian countryside has suffered in a way to wring our hearts; but our sympathy and indignation must not blind us to the fact that even in this case there has been a real advance during the last three hundred years and that such things as were done to Magdeburg and Wexford and Drogheda and the entire Palatinate in the seventeenth century are no longer possible.

There is every reason to feel dissatisfied with the slow progress that has been made in putting a stop to wrong-doing; it is our bounden

duty now to act so as to secure redress for wrong-doing; but nevertheless we must also recognize the fact that some progress has been made,
and that there is now a good deal of real sentiment, and some efficient
sentiment, against international wrong-doing. There has been a real
growth toward international peace, justice, and fair dealing. We have
still a long way to go before reaching the goal, but at least we have gone
forward a little way toward the goal. This growth will continue. We
must do everything that we can to make it continue. But we must not
blind ourselves to the fact that as yet this growth is not such as in any
shape or way to warrant us in relying for our ultimate safety in great
national crises upon anything except the strong fibre of our national
character, and upon such preparation in advance as will give that character adequate instruments wherewith to make proof of its strength.

Chapter VI

The Peace of Righteousness

"Come, Peace! not like a mourner bowed
    For honor lost and dear ones wasted,
But proud, to meet a people proud,
    With eyes that tell o' triumph tasted!
Come, with han' gripping on the hilt,
    An' step that proves ye Victory's daughter!
Longin' for you, our sperits wilt
    Like shipwrecked men's on raf's for water.

"Come, while our country feels the lift
    Of a great instinct shouting 'Forwards!'
An' knows that freedom ain't a gift
    Thet tarries long in han's of cowards!
Come, sech ez mothers prayed for, when
    They kissed their cross with lips that quivered,
An' bring fair wages for brave men,
    A nation saved, a race delivered!"

These are the noble lines of a noble poet, written in the sternest days of the great Civil War, when the writer, Lowell, was one among the millions of men who mourned the death in battle of kinsfolk dear to him. No man ever lived who hated an unjust war more than Lowell or who loved with more passionate fervor the peace of righteousness. Yet, like the other great poets of his day and country, like Holmes, who sent his own son to the war, like gentle Longfellow and the Quaker Whittier, he abhorred unrighteousness and ignoble peace more than war. These men had lofty souls. They possessed the fighting edge, without which no man is really great; for in the really great man there must be both the heart of gold and the temper of steel.

In 1864 there were in the North some hundreds of thousands of men who praised peace as the supreme end, as a good more important than all other goods, and who denounced war as the worst of all evils. These men one and all assailed and denounced Abraham Lincoln, and all voted against him for President. Moreover, at that time there were many individuals in England and France who said it was the duty of those two nations to mediate between the North and the South, so as to stop the terrible loss of life and destruction of property which attended our Civil War; and they asserted that any Americans who in such event refused to accept their mediation and to stop the war would thereby show themselves the enemies of peace. Nevertheless, Abraham Lincoln and the men back of him by their attitude prevented all such effort at mediation, declaring that they would regard it as an unfriendly act to the United States. Looking back from a distance of fifty years, we can now see clearly that Abraham Lincoln and his supporters were right. Such mediation would have been a hostile act, not only to the United States but to humanity. The men who clamored for unrighteous peace fifty years ago this fall were the enemies of mankind.

These facts should be pondered by the well-meaning men who always clamor for peace without regard to whether peace brings justice or injustice. Very many of the men and women who are at times misled into demanding peace, as if it were itself an end instead of being a means of righteousness, are men of good intelligence and sound heart who only need seriously to consider the facts, and who can then be trusted to think aright and act aright. There is, however, an element of a certain numerical importance among our people, including the members of the ultrapacificist group, who by their teachings do some real, although limited, mischief. They are a feeble folk, these ultrapacificists, morally and physically; but in a country where voice and vote are alike free, they may, if their teachings are not disregarded, create a condition of things where the crop they have sowed in folly and weakness will be reaped with blood and bitter tears by the brave men and high-hearted women of the nation.

The folly preached by some of these individuals is somewhat startling, and if it were translated from words into deeds it would constitute a crime against the nation. One professed teacher of morality made the plea in so many words that we ought to follow the example of China and deprive ourselves of all power to repel foreign attack. Surely this writer must have possessed the exceedingly small amount of information necessary in order to know that nearly half of China was under foreign dominion and that while he was writing the Germans and Japanese were battling on Chinese territory and domineering as conquerors over the Chinese in that territory. Think of the abject soul of a man capable of holding up to the admiration of free-born American citizens such a condition of serfage under alien rule!

Nor is the folly confined only to the male sex. A number of women teachers in Chicago are credited with having proposed, in view of the war, hereafter to prohibit in the teaching of history any reference to war and battles. Intellectually, of course, such persons show themselves unfit to be retained as teachers a single day, and indeed unfit to be pupils in any school more advanced than a kindergarten. But it is not their intellectual, it is also their moral shortcomings which are striking. The suppression of the truth is, of course, as grave an offense against morals as is the suggestion of the false or even the lie direct; and these teachers actually propose to teach untruths to their pupils.

True teachers of history must tell the facts of history; and if they do not tell the facts both about the wars that were righteous and the wars that were unrighteous, and about the causes that led to these wars and to success or defeat in them, they show themselves morally unfit to train the minds of boys and girls. If in addition to telling the facts they draw the lessons that should be drawn from the facts, they will give their pupils a horror of all wars that are entered into wantonly or with levity or in a spirit of mere brutal aggression or save under dire necessity. But they will also teach that among the noblest deeds of mankind are those that have been done in great wars for liberty, in wars of self-defense, in wars for the relief of oppressed peoples, in wars for putting an end to wrong-doing in the dark places of the globe.

Any teachers, in school or college, who occupied the position that these foolish, foolish teachers have sought to take, would be forever estopped from so much as mentioning Washington and Lincoln; because their lives are forever associated with great wars for righteousness. These teachers would be forever estopped from so much as mentioning the shining names of Marathon and Salamis. They would seek to blind their pupils' eyes to the glory held in the deeds and deaths of Joan of Arc, of Andreas Hofer, of Alfred the Great, of Arnold von Winkelried, of Kosciusko and Rákóczy. They would be obliged to warn their pupils against ever reading Schiller's "William Tell" or the poetry of Koerner. Such men are deaf to the lament running:

"Oh, why, Patrick Sarsfield, did we let your ships sail,
Across the dark waters from green Innisfail?"

To them Holmes's ballad of Bunker Hill and Whittier's "Laus Deo," MacMaster's "Ode to the Old Continentals" and O'Hara's "Bivouac of the Dead" are meaningless. Their cold and timid hearts are not stirred by the surge of the tremendous "Battle Hymn of the Republic." On them lessons of careers like those of Timoleon and John Hampden are lost; in their eyes the lofty self-abnegation of Robert Lee and Stonewall Jackson was folly; their dull senses do not thrill to the deathless deaths of the men who died at Thermopylæ and at the Alamo – the fight of those grim Texans of which it was truthfully said that Thermopylæ had its messengers of death but the Alamo had none.

It has actually been proposed by some of these shivering apostles of the gospel of national abjectness that, in view of the destruction that has fallen on certain peaceful powers of Europe, we should abandon all efforts at self-defense, should stop building battle-ships, and cease to take any measures to defend ourselves if attacked. It is difficult seriously to consider such a proposition. It is precisely and exactly as if the inhabitants of a village in whose neighborhood highway robberies had occurred should propose to meet the crisis by depriving the local policeman of his revolver and club.

There are, however, many high-minded people who do not agree with these extremists, but who nevertheless need to be enlightened as to the actual facts. These good people, who are busy people and not able to devote much time to thoughts about international affairs, are often confused by men whose business it is to know better. For example, a few weeks ago these good people were stirred to a moment's belief that something had been accomplished by the enactment at Washington of a score or two of all-inclusive arbitration treaties; being not unnaturally misled by the fact that those responsible for the passage of the treaties indulged in some not wholly harmless bleating as to the good effects they would produce. As a matter of fact, they *probably* will not produce the smallest effect of any kind or sort. Yet it is *possible* they may have a mischievous effect, inasmuch as under certain circumstances to fulfil them would cause frightful disaster to the United States, while to break them, even although under compulsion and because it was absolutely necessary, would be fruitful of keen humiliation to every right-thinking man who is jealous of our international good name.

If for example, whatever the outcome of the present war, a great triumphant military despotism declared that it would not recognize the Monroe Doctrine or seized Magdalena Bay, or one of the Dutch West Indies, or the Island of St. Thomas, and fortified it; or if – as would be quite possible – it announced that we had no right to fortify the Isthmus of Panama, and itself landed on adjacent territory to erect similar fortifications; then, under these absurd treaties, we would be obliged, if we happened to have made one of them with one of the countries involved, to go into an interminable discussion of the subject before a joint commission, while the hostile nation proceeded to make its position impregnable. It seems incredible that the United States government could have made such treaties; but it has just done so, with the warm approval of the professional pacificists.

These treaties were entered into when the administration had before its eyes at that very moment the examples of Belgium and Luxembourg, which showed beyond possibility of doubt, especially when taken in connection with other similar incidents that have occurred during the last couple of decades, that there are various great military empires in the Old World who will pay not one moment's heed to the most solemn and binding treaty, if it is to their interest to break it. If any one of these empires, as the result of the present contest, obtains something approaching to a position of complete predominance in the Old World, it is absolutely certain that it would pay no heed whatever to these treaties, if it desired to better its position in the New World by taking possession of the Dutch or Danish West Indies or of the territory of some weak American state on the mainland of the continent.

In such event we would be obliged either instantly ourselves to repudiate the scandalous treaties by which the government at Washington has just sought to tie our hands – and thereby expose ourselves in our turn to the charge of bad faith – or else we should have to abdicate our position as a great power and submit to abject humiliation.

Since these articles of mine were written and published, I am glad to see that James Bryce, a lifelong advocate of peace and the stanchest possible friend of the United States, has taken precisely the position herein taken. He dwells, as I have dwelt, upon the absolute need of protecting small states that behave themselves from absorption in great military empires. He insists, as I have insisted, upon the need of the reduction of armaments, the quenching of the baleful spirit of militarism, and the admission of the peoples everywhere to a fuller share in the control of foreign policy – all to be accomplished by some kind of international league of peace. He adds, however, as the culminating and most important portion of his article:

"But no scheme for preventing future wars will have any chance of success unless it rests upon the assurance that the states which enter it will loyally and steadfastly abide by it and that each and all of them will join in coercing by their overwhelming united strength any state which may disregard the obligations it has undertaken."

This is almost exactly what I have said. Indeed, it is almost word for word what I have said – an agreement which is all the more striking because when he wrote it Lord Bryce could not have known what I had written. We must insist on righteousness first and foremost. We must strive for peace always; but we must never hesitate to put righteousness above peace. In order to do this, we must put force back of righteousness, for, as the world now is, national righteousness without force back of it speedily becomes a matter of derision. To the doctrine that might makes right, it is utterly useless to oppose the doctrine of right unbacked by might.

It is not even true that what the pacificists desire is right. The leaders of the pacificists of this country who for five months now have been crying, "Peace, peace," have been too timid even to say that they want the peace to be a righteous one. We needlessly dignify such outcries when we speak of them as well-meaning. The weaklings who raise their shrill piping for a peace that shall consecrate successful wrong occupy a position quite as immoral as and infinitely more contemptible than the position of the wrong-doers themselves. The ruthless strength of the great absolutist leaders – Elizabeth of England, Catherine of Russia, Peter the Great, Frederick the Great, Napoleon, Bismarck – is certainly infinitely better for their own nations and is probably better for mankind at large than the loquacious impotence, ultimately trouble-breeding, which has recently marked our own international policy. A policy of blood and iron is sometimes very wicked; but it rarely does as much harm, and never excites as much derision, as a policy of milk and water – and it comes dangerously near flattery to call the foreign policy of the United States under President Wilson and Mr. Bryan merely one of milk and water. Strength at least commands respect; whereas the prattling feebleness that dares not rebuke any concrete wrong, and whose proposals for right are marked by sheer fatuity, is fit only to excite weeping among angels and among men the bitter laughter of scorn.

At this moment any peace which leaves unredressed the wrongs of Belgium, and which does not effectively guarantee Belgium and all other small nations that behave themselves, against the repetition of such wrongs would be a well-nigh unmixed evil. As far as we personally are concerned, such a peace would inevitably mean that we should at once and in haste have to begin to arm ourselves or be exposed in our turn to the most frightful risk of disaster. Let our people take thought for the future. What Germany did to Belgium because her need was great and because she possessed the ruthless force with which to meet her need she would, of course, do to us if her need demanded it; and in such event what her representatives now say as to her intentions toward America would trouble her as little as her signature to the neutrality treaties troubled her when she subjugated Belgium. Nor does she stand alone in her views of international morality. More than one of the great powers engaged in this war has shown by her conduct in the past that if it profited her she would without the smallest scruple treat any land in the two Americas as Belgium has been treated. What has recently happened in the Old World should be pondered deeply by the nations of the New World; by Chile, Argentina, and Brazil no less than by the United States. The world war has proved beyond peradventure that the principle underlying the Monroe Doctrine is of vast moment to the welfare of all America, and that neither this nor any other principle can be made effective save as power is put behind it.

Belgium was absolutely innocent of offense. Her cities have been laid waste or held to ransom for gigantic sums of money; her fruitful fields have been trampled into mire; her sons have died on the field of battle; her daughters are broken-hearted fugitives; a million of her people have fled to foreign lands. Entirely disregarding all accusations as to outrages on individuals, it yet remains true that disaster terrible beyond belief has befallen this peaceful nation of six million people who themselves had been guilty of not even the smallest wrong-doing. Louvain and Dinant are smoke-grimed and blood-stained ruins. Brussels has been held to enormous ransom, although it did not even strive to defend itself. Antwerp did strive to defend itself. Because soldiers in the forts attempted to repulse the enemy, hundreds of houses in the undefended city were wrecked with bombs from air-ships, and throngs of peaceful men, women, and children were driven from their homes by the sharp terror of death. Be it remembered always that not one man in Brussels, not one man in Antwerp, had even the smallest responsibility for the disaster inflicted upon them. Innocence has proved not even the smallest safeguard against such woe and suffering as we in this land can at present hardly imagine.

What befell Antwerp and Brussels will surely some day befall New York or San Francisco, and may happen to many an inland city also, if we do not shake off our supine folly, if we trust for safety to peace treaties unbacked by force. At the beginning of last month, by the appointment of the President, peace services were held in the churches of this land. As far as these services consisted of sermons and prayers of good and wise people who wished peace only if it represented righteousness, who did not desire that peace should come unless it came to consecrate justice and not wrong-doing, good and not evil, the movement represented good. In so far, however, as the movement was understood to be one for immediate peace without any regard to righteousness or justice, without any regard for righting the wrongs of those who have been crushed by unmerited disaster, then the movement represented mischief, precisely as fifty years ago, in 1864, in our own country a similar movement for peace, to be obtained by acknowledgment of disunion and by the perpetuation of slavery, would have represented mischief. In the present case, however, the mischief was confined purely to those taking part in the movement in an unworthy spirit; for (like the peace parades and newspaper peace petitions) it was a merely subjective phenomenon; it had not the slightest effect of any kind, sort, or description upon any of the combatants abroad and could not possibly have any effect upon them. It is well for our own sakes that we should pray sincerely and humbly for the peace of righteousness; but we must guard ourselves from any illusion as to the news of our having thus prayed producing the least effect upon those engaged in the war.

There is just one way in which to meet the upholders of the doctrine that might makes right. To do so we must prove that right will make might, by backing right with might.

In his second inaugural address Andrew Jackson laid down the rule by which every national American administration ought to guide itself, saying: "The foreign policy adopted by our government is to do justice to all, and to submit to wrong by none."

The statement of the dauntless old fighter of New Orleans is as true now as when he wrote it. We must stand absolutely for righteousness. But to do so is utterly without avail unless we possess the strength and the loftiness of spirit which will back righteousness with deeds and not mere words. We must clear the rubbish from off our souls and admit that everything that has been done in passing peace treaties, arbitration treaties, neutrality treaties, Hague treaties, and the like, with no sanction of force behind them, amounts to literally and absolutely zero, to literally and absolutely nothing, in any time of serious crisis. We must recognize that to enter into foolish treaties which cannot be kept is as wicked as to break treaties which can and ought to be kept. We must labor for an international agreement among the great civilized nations which shall put the full force of all of them back of any one of them, and of any well-behaved weak nation, which is wronged by any other power. Until we have completed this purpose, we must keep ourselves ready, high of heart and undaunted of soul, to back our rights with our strength.

Chapter VII

An International Posse Comitatus

Most Western Americans who are past middle age remember young, rapidly growing, and turbulent communities in which there was at first complete anarchy. During the time when there was no central police power to which to appeal every man worth his salt, in other words every man fit for existence in such a community, had to be prepared to defend himself; and usually, although not always, the fact that he was prepared saved him from all trouble, whereas unpreparedness was absolutely certain to invite disaster.

In such communities before there was a regular and fully organized police force there came an interval during which the preservation of the peace depended upon the action of a single official, a sheriff or marshal, who if the law was defied in arrogant fashion summoned a posse comitatus composed of as many armed, thoroughly efficient, law-abiding citizens as were necessary in order to put a stop to the wrong-doing. Under these conditions each man had to keep himself armed and both able and willing to respond to the call of the peace-officer; and furthermore, if he had a shred of wisdom he kept himself ready in an emergency to act on his own behalf if the peace-officer did not or could not do his duty.

In such towns I have myself more than once seen well-meaning but foolish citizens endeavor to meet the exigencies of the case by simply passing resolutions of disarmament without any power back of them. That is, they passed self-denying ordinances, saying that nobody was to carry arms; but they failed to provide methods for carrying such ordinances into effect. In every case the result was the same. Good citizens for the moment abandoned their weapons. The bad men continued to carry them. Things grew worse instead of better; and then the good men came to their senses and clothed some representative of the police with power to employ force, potential or existing, against the wrong-doers.

Affairs in the international world are at this time in analogous condition. There is no central police power, and not the least likelihood of its being created. Well-meaning enthusiasts have tried their hands to an almost unlimited extent in the way of devising all-inclusive arbitration treaties, neutrality treaties, disarmament proposals, and the like, with no force back of them, and the result has been stupendous and discreditable failure. Preparedness for war on the part of individual nations has sometimes but not always averted war. Unpreparedness for war, as in the case of China, Korea, and Luxembourg, has invariably invited smashing disaster, and sometimes complete conquest. Surely these conditions should teach a lesson that any man who runs may read unless his eyes have been blinded by folly or his heart weakened by cowardice.

The immediately vital lesson for each individual nation is that as things are now it must in time of crisis rely on its own stout hearts and ready hands for self-defense. Existing treaties are utterly worthless so far as concerns protecting any free, well-behaved people from one of the great aggressive military monarchies of the world. The all-inclusive arbitration treaties such as those recently negotiated by Messrs. Wilson and Bryan, when taken in connection with our refusal to act under existing treaties, represent about the highest point of slightly mischievous fatuity which can be attained in international matters. Inasmuch as we ourselves are the power that initiated their negotiation, we can do our plain duty to ourselves and our neighbors only by ourselves proceeding from the outset on the theory, and by warning our neighbors, that these treaties in any time of crisis will certainly not be respected by any serious adversary, and probably will of necessity be violated by ourselves. They do not in even the very smallest degree relieve us of the necessity of preparedness for war. To this point of our duty to be prepared I will return later.

But we ought not to and must not rest content merely with working for our own defense. The utterly appalling calamity that has befallen the civilized world during the last five months, and, above all, the horrible catastrophe that has overwhelmed Belgium without Belgium's having the smallest responsibility in the matter, must make the least thoughtful realize how unsatisfactory is the present basis of international relations among civilized powers. In order to make things better several things are necessary. We must clearly grasp the fact that mere selfish avoidance of duty to others, even although covered by such fine words as "peace" and "neutrality," is a wretched thing and an obstacle to securing the peace of righteousness throughout the world. We must recognize clearly the old common-law doctrine that a right without a remedy is void. We must firmly grasp the fact that measures should be taken to put force back of good faith in the observance of treaties. The worth of treaties depends purely upon the good faith with which they are executed; and it is mischievous folly to enter into treaties without providing for their execution and wicked folly to enter into them if they ought not to be executed.

It is necessary to devise means for putting the collective and efficient strength of all the great powers of civilization back of any well-behaved power which is wronged by another power. In other words, we must devise means for executing treaties in good faith, by the establishment of some great international tribunal, and by securing the enforcement of the decrees of this tribunal through the action of a posse comitatus of powerful and civilized nations, all of them being bound by solemn agreement to coerce any power that offends against the decrees of the tribunal. That there will be grave difficulties in successfully working out this plan I would be the first to concede, and I would be the first to insist that to work it out successfully would be impossible unless the nations acted in good faith. But the plan is feasible, and it is the only one which at the moment offers any chance of success. Ever since the days of Henry IV of France there has been a growth, slow and halting to be sure but yet evidently a growth, in recognition by the public conscience of civilized nations that there should be a method of making the rules of international morality obligatory and binding among the powers. But merely to trust to public opinion without organized force back of it is silly. Force must be put back of justice, and nations must not shrink from the duty of proceeding by any means that are necessary against wrong-doers. It is the failure to recognize these vital truths that has rendered the actions of our government during the last few years impotent to preserve world peace and fruitful only in earning for us the half-veiled derision of other nations.

The attitude of the present administration during the last five months shows how worthless the present treaties, unbacked by force, are, and how utterly ineffective mere passive neutrality is to secure even the smallest advance in world morality. I have been very reluctant in any way to criticise the action of the present administration in foreign affairs; I have faithfully, and in some cases against my own deep-rooted personal convictions, sought to justify what it has done in Mexico and as regards the present war; but the time has come when loyalty to the administration's action in foreign affairs means disloyalty to our national self-interest and to our obligations toward humanity at large. As regards Belgium the administration has clearly taken the ground that our own selfish ease forbids us to fulfil our explicit obligations to small neutral states when they are deeply wronged. It will never be possible in any war to commit a clearer breach of international morality than that committed by Germany in the invasion and subjugation of Belgium. Every one of the nations involved in this war, and the United States as well, have committed such outrages in the past. But the very purpose of the Hague conventions and of all similar international agreements was to put a stop to such misconduct in the future.

At the outset I ask our people to remember that what I say is based on the assumption that we are bound in good faith to fulfil our treaty obligations; that we will neither favor nor condemn any other nation except on the ground of its behavior; that we feel as much good-will to the people of Germany or Austria as to the people of England, of France, or of Russia; that we speak for Belgium only as we could speak for Holland or Switzerland or one of the Scandinavian or Balkan nations; and that if the circumstances as regards Belgium had been reversed we would have protested as emphatically against wrong action by England or France as we now protest against wrong action by Germany.

The United States and the great powers now at war were parties to the international code treated in the regulations annexed to the Hague conventions of 1899 and 1907. As President, acting on behalf of this government, and in accordance with the unanimous wish of our people, I ordered the signature of the United States to these conventions.

Most emphatically I would not have permitted such a farce to have gone through if it had entered my head that this government would not consider itself bound to do all it could to see that the regulations to which it made itself a party were actually observed when the necessity for their observance arose. I cannot imagine any sensible nation thinking it worth while to sign future Hague conventions if even such a powerful neutral as the United States does not care enough about them to protest against their open breach. Of the present neutral powers the United States of America is the most disinterested and the strongest, and should therefore bear the main burden of responsibility in this matter.

It is quite possible to make an argument to the effect that we never should have entered into the Hague conventions, because our sole duty is to ourselves and not to others, and our sole concern should be to keep ourselves at peace, at any cost, and not to help other powers that are oppressed, and not to protest against wrong-doing. I do not myself accept this view; but in practice it is the view taken by the present administration, apparently with at the moment the approval of the mass of our people. Such a policy, while certainly not exalted, and in my judgment neither far-sighted nor worthy of a high-spirited and lofty-souled nation, is yet in a sense understandable, and in a sense defensible.

But it is quite indefensible to make agreements and not live up to them. The climax of absurdity is for any administration to do what the present administration during the last five months has done. Mr. Wilson's administration has shirked doing the duty plainly imposed on it by the obligations of the conventions already entered into; and at the same time it has sought to obtain cheap credit by entering into a couple of score new treaties infinitely more drastic than the old ones, and quite impossible of honest fulfilment. When the Belgian people complained of violations of the Hague tribunal, it was a mockery, it was a timid and unworthy abandonment of duty on our part, for President Wilson to refer them back to the Hague court, when he knew that the Hague court was less than a shadow unless the United States by doing its clear duty gave the Hague court some substance. If the Hague conventions represented nothing but the expression of feeble aspirations toward decency, uttered only in time of profound peace, and not to be even expressed above a whisper when with awful bloodshed and suffering the conventions were broken, then it was idle folly to enter into them. If, on the other hand, they meant anything, if the United States had a serious purpose, a serious sense of its obligations to world righteousness, when it entered into them, then its plain duty as the trustee of civilization is to investigate the charges solemnly made as to the violation of the Hague conventions. If such investigation is made, and if the charges prove well founded, then it is the duty of the United States to take whatever action may be necessary to vindicate the principles of international law set forth in these conventions.

I am not concerned with the charges of individual atrocity. The prime fact is that Belgium committed no offense whatever, and yet that her territory has been invaded and her people subjugated. This prime fact cannot be left out of consideration in dealing with any matter that has occurred in connection with it. Her neutrality has certainly been violated, and this is in clear violation of the fundamental principles of the Hague conventions. It appears clear that undefended towns have been bombarded, and that towns which were defended have been attacked with bombs at a time when no attack was made upon the defenses. This is certainly in contravention of the Hague agreement forbidding the bombardment of undefended towns. Illegal and excessive contributions are expressly condemned under Articles 49 and 52 of the conventions. If these articles do not forbid the levying of such sums as $40,000,000 from Brussels and $90,000,000 from the province of Brabant, then the articles are absolutely meaningless. Articles 43 and 50 explicitly forbid the infliction of a collective penalty, pecuniary or otherwise, on a population on account of acts of individuals for which it cannot be regarded as collectively responsible. Either this prohibition is meaningless or it prohibits just such acts as the punitive destruction of Visé, Louvain, Aerschot, and Dinant. Furthermore, a great deal of the appalling devastation of central and eastern Belgium has been apparently terrorizing and not punitive in its purpose, and this is explicitly forbidden by the Hague conventions.

Now, it may be that there is an explanation and justification for a portion of what has been done. But if the Hague conventions mean anything, and if bad faith in the observation of treaties is not to be treated with cynical indifference, then the United States government should inform itself as to the facts, and should take whatever action is necessary in reference thereto. The extent to which the action should go may properly be a subject for discussion. But that there should be some action is beyond discussion; unless, indeed, we ourselves are content to take the view that treaties, conventions, and international engagements and agreements of all kinds are to be treated by us and by everybody else as what they have been authoritatively declared to be, "scraps of paper," the writing on which is intended for no better purpose than temporarily to amuse the feeble-minded.

If the above statements seem in the eyes of my German friends hostile to Germany, let me emphasize the fact that they are predicated upon a course of action which if extended and applied as it should be extended and applied would range the United States on the side of Germany if any such assault were made upon Germany as has been made upon Belgium, or if either Belgium or any of the other allies committed similar wrong-doing. Many Germans assert and believe that if Germany had not acted as she did France and England would have invaded Belgium and have committed similar wrongs. In such case it would have been our clear duty to behave toward them exactly as we ought now to behave toward Germany. But the fact that other powers might under other conditions do wrong, affords no justification for failure to act on the wrong that has actually been committed. It must always be kept in mind, however, that we cannot expect the nation against whose actions we protest to accept our position as warranted, unless we make it clear that we have both the will and the power to interfere on behalf of that nation if in its turn it is oppressed. In other words, we must show that we believe in right and therefore in living up to our promises in good faith; and, furthermore, that we are both able and ready to put might behind right.

As I have before said, I think that the party in Germany which believes in a policy of aggression represents but a minority of the nation. It is powerful only because the great majority of the German people are rightfully in fear of aggression at the expense of Germany, and sanction striking only because they fear lest they themselves be struck. The greatest service that could be rendered to peace would be to convince Germany, as well as other powers, that in such event we would do all we could on behalf of the power that was wronged. Extremists in England, France, and Russia talk as if the proper outcome of the present war would be the utter dismemberment of Germany and her reduction to impotence such as that which followed for her upon the Thirty Years' War. I have actually received letters from Frenchmen and Englishmen upbraiding me for what they regard as a pro-German leaning in these articles I have written. To these well-meaning persons I can only say that Americans who remember the extreme bitterness felt by Northerners for Southerners, and Southerners for Northerners, at the end of the Civil War, are saddened but in no wise astonished that other peoples should show a like bitterness. I can only repeat that to dismember and hopelessly shatter Germany would be a frightful calamity for mankind, precisely as the dismemberment and shattering of the British Empire or of the French Republic would be. It is right that the United States should regard primarily its own interests. But I believe that I speak for a considerable number of my countrymen when I say that we ought not solely to consider our own interests. Above all, we should not do as the present administration does; for it refuses to take any concrete action in favor of any nation which is wronged; and yet it also refuses to act so that we may ourselves be sufficient for our own protection.

We ought not to trust in words unbacked by deeds. We should be able to defend ourselves. We should also be ready and able to join in preventing the infliction of disaster of the kind of which I speak upon any civilized power, great or small, whether it be at the present time Belgium, or at some future day Germany or England, Holland, Sweden or Hungary, Russia or Japan.

So much for questions of international right, and of our duty to others in international affairs. Now for our duty to ourselves.

A sincere desire to act well toward other nations must not blind us to the fact that as yet the standard of international morality is both low and irregular. The behavior of the great military empires of the Old World, in reference to their treaty obligations and their moral obligations toward countries such as Belgium, Finland, and Korea, shows that it would be utter folly for us in any grave crisis to trust to anything save our own preparedness and resolution for our safety. The other day there appeared in the newspapers extracts from a translation of a report made by an officer of the Prussian army staff outlining the plan of operations by Germany in the event of war with America. Great surprise was expressed by innocent Americans that such plans should be in existence, and certain gentlemen who speak for Germany denied that the report (which was printed and openly sold in Germany in pamphlet form) was "official." Neither the resentment expressed nor yet the denials were necessary. One feature of the admirable preparedness in which Germany and Japan stand so far above all other nations, and especially above our own, is their careful consideration of hostilities with all possible antagonists. Bernhardi's famous books treat of possible war with Austria, and possible attack by Austria upon Germany, although the prime lessons that they teach are those contained in the possibility of war as it has actually occurred, with Germany and Austria in alliance. This does not indicate German hostility to Austria; it merely indicates German willingness to look squarely in the face all possible facts. Of course, and quite properly, the German General Staff has carefully considered the question of hostilities with America, and, of course, plans were drawn up with minute care and prevision at the time when there was friction between the two countries over Samoa, at the time when Admiral Dietrich clashed with Dewey in Manila Bay, and on the later occasion when there was friction in connection with Venezuela. This did not represent any special German ill will toward America. It represented the common-sense – albeit somewhat cold-blooded – consideration of possibilities by Germany's rulers; and the failure to give this consideration would have reflected severely upon these rulers – although I do not regard some of the actions proposed as proper from the standpoint of warfare as the United States has practised it. To become angry because such plans exist would be childish. To fail to profit by our knowledge that they certainly do exist would however, be not merely childish but imbecile. I have myself become personally cognizant of the existence of such plans for operations against us, and of the larger features of their details, in two cases, affecting two different nations.

The essential feature of these plans was (and doubtless is) the seizure of some of our great coast cities and the terrorization of these cities so as to make them give enormous ransoms; ransoms of such size that our own country would be crippled, whereas our foes would be enabled to run the war against us with a handsome profit to themselves. These plans are based, of course, upon the belief that we have not sufficient foresight and intelligence to keep our navy in first-class condition, and upon not merely the belief but the knowledge that our regular army is so small and our utter unpreparedness otherwise so great that on land we would be entirely helpless against a moderate-sized expeditionary force belonging to any first-class military power. Foreign military and naval observers know well that our navy has been used during the last eighteen months in connection with the Mexican situation in such manner as to accomplish the minimum of results as regards Mexico, while at the same time to do the maximum of damage in interrupting the manœuvring and the gun practice of our fleets. They regard Messrs. Wilson and Bryan as representative of the American people in their entire inability to understand the real nature of the forces that underlie international relations and the importance of preparedness. They are entirely cold-blooded in their views of us. Foreign rulers may despise us for our supine unpreparedness, and for our readiness to make treaties, taken together with our refusal to fulfil these treaties by seeking to avert wrong done to others. But their contempt will not prevent their using this nation as arbiter in order to bring about peace if to do so suits their purposes; and if, on the contrary, one or the other of the several great military empires becomes the world mistress as the result of this war, that power will infringe our rights whenever and to the extent that it deems it advantageous to do so, and will make war upon us whenever it believes that such war will be to its own advantage.

In the event of such a war against us it is well to remember that the spiritless and selfish type of neutrality which we have observed in the present war will be remembered by all other nations on whichever side they have been engaged in this contest, and will give each of them more or less satisfaction in the event of disaster befalling us. These nations, if they come to a deadlock as the result of this war, will not be withheld by any sentiment of indignation against or contempt for us from utilizing the services of the President as a medium for bringing about peace, if this seems the most convenient method of getting peace. But, whether they do this or not, they will retain a smouldering ill will toward us, one and all of them; and if we were assailed it would be utterly quixotic, utterly foolish of any one of them to come to our aid no matter what wrongs were inflicted upon us. It would be quite impossible for any power to treat us worse than Belgium has been treated by Germany or to attack us with less warrant than was shown when Belgium was attacked. Bombs have been continually dropped by the Germans in the city of Paris and in other cities, wrecking private houses and killing men, women, and children at a time when there was no pretense that any military attacks were being made upon the cities, or that any other object was served than that of terrorizing the civilian population. Cities have been destroyed and others held to huge ransom. All these practices are forbidden by the Hague conventions. Inasmuch as we have not made a single protest against them when other powers have suffered, it would be both ridiculous and humiliating for us to make even the slightest appeal for assistance or to expect any assistance from any other powers if ever we in our turn suffer in like fashion. It would be purely our affair. We would have no right to expect that other powers would take the kind of action which we ourselves have refused to take. It would be our time to take our medicine, and it would be folly and cowardice to make wry faces over it or to expect sympathy, still less aid, from outsiders. As I have already stated, my own view is most strongly that, if we are assailed in accordance with the plans of foreign powers above mentioned, it would be our business positively to refuse to allow any city to ransom itself, and sternly to accept the destruction of New York, or San Francisco, or any other city as the alternative of such ransom. Our duty would be to accept these disasters as the payment rightfully due from us to fate for our folly in having listened to the clamor of the feeble folk among the ultrapacificists, and in having indorsed the unspeakable silliness of the policy contained in the proposed all-inclusive arbitration treaties of Mr. Taft and in the accomplished all-inclusive arbitration treaties of Messrs. Wilson and Bryan.

I very earnestly hope that this nation will ultimately adopt a dignified and self-respecting policy in international affairs. I earnestly hope that ultimately we shall live up to every international obligation we have undertaken – exactly as we did live up to them during the seven and a half years while I was President. I earnestly hope that we shall ourselves become one of the joint guarantors of world peace under such a plan as that I in this book outline, and that we shall hold ourselves ready and willing to act as a member of the international posse comitatus to enforce the peace of righteousness as against any offender big or small. This would mean a great practical stride toward relief from the burden of excessive military preparation. It would mean that a long step had been taken toward at least minimizing and restricting the area and extent of possible warfare. It would mean that all liberty-loving and enlightened peoples, great and small, would be freed from the haunting nightmare of terror which now besets them when they think of the possible conquest of their land.

Until this can be done we owe it to ourselves as a nation effectively to safeguard ourselves against all likelihood of disaster at the hands of a foreign foe. We should bring our navy up to the highest point of preparedness, we should handle it purely from military considerations, and should see that the training was never intermitted. We should make our little regular army larger and more effective than at present. We should provide for it an adequate reserve. In addition, I most heartily believe that we should return to the ideal held by our people in the days of Washington although never lived up to by them. We should follow the example of such typical democracies as Switzerland and Australia and provide and require military training for all our young men. Switzerland's efficient army has unquestionably been the chief reason why in this war there has been no violation of her neutrality. Australia's system of military training has enabled her at once to ship large bodies of first-rate fighting men to England's aid. Our northern neighbors have done even better than Australia; perhaps special mention should be made of St. John, Newfoundland, which has sent to the front one in five of her adult male population, a larger percentage than any other city of the empire; a feat probably due to the fact that in practically all her schools there is good military training, while her young men have much practice in shooting tournaments. England at the moment is saved from the fate of Belgium only because of her navy; and the small size of her army, her lack of arms, her lack of previous preparations doubtless afford the chief reason why this war has occurred at all at this time. There would probably have been no war if England had followed the advice so often urged on her by the lamented Lord Roberts, for in that case she would have been able immediately to put in the field an army as large and effective as, for instance, that of France.

Training of our young men in field manœuvres and in marksmanship, as is done in Switzerland, and to a slightly less extent in Australia, would be of immense advantage to the physique and morale of our whole population. It would not represent any withdrawal of our population from civil pursuits, such as occurs among the great military states of the European Continent. In Switzerland, for instance, the ground training is given in the schools, and the young man after graduating serves only some four months with the branch of the army to which he is attached, and after that only about eight days a year, not counting his rifle practice. All serve alike, rich and poor, without any exceptions; and all whom I have ever met, the poor even more than the rich, are enthusiastic over the beneficial effects of the service and the increase in self-reliance, self-respect, and efficiency which it has brought. The utter worthlessness of make-believe soldiers who have not been trained, and who are improvised on the Wilson-Bryan theory, will be evident to any one who cares to read such works as Professor Johnson's recent volume on Bull Run. Our people should make a thorough study of the Swiss and Australian systems, and then adapt them to our own use. To do so would not be a stride toward war, as the feeble folk among the ultra-pacificists would doubtless maintain. It would be the most effectual possible guarantee that peace would dwell within our borders; and it would also make it possible for us not only to insure peace for ourselves, but to have our words carry weight if we spoke against the commission of wrong and injustice at the expense of others.

But we must always remember that no institutions will avail unless the private citizen has the right spirit. When a leading congressman, himself with war experience, shows conclusively in open speech in the House that we are utterly unprepared to do our duty to ourselves if assailed, President Wilson answers him with a cheap sneer, with unworthy levity; and the repeated warnings of General Wood are treated with the same indifference. Nevertheless, I do not believe that this attitude on the part of our public servants really represents the real convictions of the average American. The ideal citizen of a free state must have in him the stuff which in time of need will enable him to show himself a first-class fighting man who scorns either to endure or to inflict wrong. American society is sound at core and this means that at bottom we, as a people, accept as the basis of sound morality not slothful ease and soft selfishness and the loud timidity that fears every species of risk and hardship, but the virile strength of manliness which clings to the ideal of stern, unflinching performance of duty, and which follows whithersoever that ideal may lead.

Chapter VIII

Self-Defense without Militarism

The other day one of the typical ultrapacificists or peace-at-any-price men put the ultrapacificist case quite clearly, both in a statement of his own and by a quotation of what he called the "golden words" of Mr. Bryan at Mohonk. In arguing that we should under no conditions fight for our rights, and that we should make no preparation whatever to secure ourselves against wrong, this writer pointed out China as the proper model for America. He did this on the ground that China, which did not fight, was yet "older" than Rome, Greece, and Germany, which had fought, and that its example was therefore to be preferred.

This, of course, is a position which saves the need of argument. If the average American wants to be a Chinaman, if China represents his ideal, then he should by all means follow the advice of pacificists like the writer in question and be a supporter of Mr. Bryan. If any man seriously believes that China has played a nobler and more useful part in the world than Athens and Rome and Germany, then he is quite right to try to Chinafy the United States. In such event he must of course believe that all the culture, all the literature, all the art, all the political and cultural liberty and social well-being, which modern Europe and the two Americas have inherited from Rome and Greece, and that all that has been done by Germany from the days of Charlemagne to the present time, represent mere error and confusion. He must believe that the average German or Frenchman or Englishman or inhabitant of North or South America occupies a lower moral, intellectual, and physical status than the average coolie who with his fellows composes the overwhelming majority of the Chinese population. To my mind such a proposition is unfit for debate outside of certain types of asylum. But those who sincerely take the view that this gentleman takes are unquestionably right in copying China in every detail, and nothing that I can say will appeal to them.

The "golden words" of Mr. Bryan were as follows:

> I believe that this nation could stand before the world to-day and tell the world that it did not believe in war, that it did not believe that it was the right way to settle disputes, that it had no disputes which it was not willing to submit to the judgment of the world. If this nation did that, it not only would not be attacked by any other nation on the earth, but it would become the supreme power in the world.

Of course, it is to be assumed that Mr. Bryan means what he says. If he does, then he is willing to submit to arbitration the question whether the Japanese have or have not the right to send unlimited numbers of immigrants to this shore. If Mr. Bryan does not mean this, among other specific things, then the "golden words" in question represent merely the emotionalism of the professional orator. Of course if Mr. Bryan means what he says, he also believes that we should not have interfered in Cuba and that Cuba ought now to be the property of Spain. He also believes that we ought to have permitted Colombia to reconquer and deprive of their independence the people of Panama, and that we should not have built the Panama Canal. He also believes that California and Texas ought now to be parts of Mexico, enjoying whatever blessings complete abstinence from foreign war has secured that country during the last three years. He also believes that the Declaration of Independence was an arbitrable matter and that the United States ought now to be a dependency of Great Britain. Unless Mr. Bryan does believe all of these things then his "golden words" represent only a rhetorical flourish. He is Secretary of State and the right-hand man of President Wilson, and President Wilson is completely responsible for whatever he says and for the things he does – or rather which he leaves undone.

Now, it is quite useless for me to write with any view to convincing gentlemen like Mr. Bryan and the writer in question. If they really do represent our fellow countrymen, then they are right in holding up China as our ideal; not the modern China, not the China that is changing and moving forward, but old China. In such event Americans ought frankly to class themselves with the Chinese. That is where, on this theory, they belong. If this is so, then let us fervently pray that the Japanese or Germans or some other virile people that does not deify moral, mental, and physical impotence, may speedily come to rule over us.

I am, however, writing on the assumption that Americans are still on the whole like their forefathers who followed Washington, and like their fathers who fought in the armies of Grant and Lee. I am writing on the assumption that, even though temporarily misled, they will not permanently and tamely submit to oppression, and that they will ultimately think intelligently as to what they should do to safeguard themselves against aggression. I abhor unjust war, and I deplore that the need even for just war should ever occur. I believe we should set our faces like flint against any policy of aggression by this country on the rights of any other country. But I believe that we should look facts in the face. I believe that it is unworthy weakness to fear to face the truth. Moreover, I believe that we should have in us that fibre of manhood which will make us follow duty whithersoever it may lead. Unquestionably, we should render all the service it is in our power to render to righteousness. To do this we must be able to back righteousness with force, to put might back of right. It may well be that by following out this theory we can in the end do our part in conjunction with other nations of the world to bring about, if not – as I hope – a world peace, yet at least an important minimizing of the chances for war and of the areas of possible war. But meanwhile it is absolutely our duty to prepare for our own defense.

This country needs something like the Swiss system of war training for its young men. Switzerland is one of the most democratic governments in the world, and it has given its young men such an efficient training as to insure entire preparedness for war, without suffering from the least touch of militarism. Switzerland is at peace now primarily because all the great military nations that surround it know that its people have no intention of making aggression on anybody and yet that they are thoroughly prepared to hold their own and are resolute to fight to the last against any invader who attempts either to subjugate their territory or by violating its neutrality to make it a battle-ground.

A bishop of the Episcopal Church recently wrote me as follows:

> How lamentable that we should stand idle, making no preparations to enforce peace, and crying "peace" when there is none! I have scant sympathy for the shortsightedness of those who decry preparation for war as a means of preventing it.

The manager of a land company in Alabama writes me urging that some one speak for reasonable preparedness on the part of the nation. He states that it is always possible that we shall be engaged in hostilities with some first-class power, that he hopes and believes that war will never come, but adds:

> I may not believe that my home will burn down or that I am going to die within the period of my expectancy, but nevertheless I carry fire and life insurance to the full insurable value on my property and on my life to the extent of my ability. The only insurance of our liberties as a people is full preparation for a defense adequate against any attack and made in time to fully meet any attack. We do not *know* the attack is coming; but to wait until it does come will be too late. Our present weakness lies in the wide-spread opinion among our people that this country is invincible because of its large population and vast resources. This I believe is true if, and only if, we use these resources or a small part of them to protect the major part, and if we train at least a part of our people how to defend the nation. Under existing conditions we can hardly hope to have an effective army in the field in less time than eight or ten months. To-day not one per cent of our people know anything about rifle shooting.

I quote these two out of many letters, because they sum up the general feeling of men of vision. Both of my correspondents are most sincerely for peace. No man can possibly be more anxious for peace than I am. I ask those individuals who think of me as a firebrand to remember that during the seven and a half years I was President not a shot was fired at any soldier of a hostile nation by any American soldier or sailor, and there was not so much as a threat of war. Even when the state of Panama threw off the alien yoke of Colombia and when this nation, acting as was its manifest duty, by recognizing Panama as an independent state stood for the right of the governed to govern themselves on the Isthmus, as well as for justice and humanity, there was not a shot fired by any of our people at any Colombian. The blood recently shed at Vera Cruz, like the unpunished wrongs recently committed on our people in Mexico, had no parallel during my administration. When I left the presidency there was not a cloud on the horizon – and one of the reasons why there was not a cloud on the horizon was that the American battle fleet had just returned from its sixteen months' trip around the world, a trip such as no other battle fleet of any power had ever taken, which it had not been supposed could be taken, and which exercised a greater influence for peace than all the peace congresses of the last fifty years. With Lowell I most emphatically believe that peace is not a gift that tarries long in the hands of cowards; and the fool and the weakling are no improvement on the coward.

Nineteen centuries ago in the greatest of all books we were warned that whoso loses his life for righteousness shall save it and that he who seeks to save it shall lose it. The ignoble and abject gospel of those who would teach us that it is preferable to endure disgrace and discredit than to run any risk to life or limb would defeat its own purpose; for that kind of submission to wrong-doing merely invites further wrong-doing, as has been shown a thousand times in history and as is shown by the case of China in our own days. Moreover, our people, however ill-prepared, would never consent to such abject submission; and indeed as a matter of fact our publicists and public men and our newspapers, instead of being too humble and submissive, are only too apt to indulge in very offensive talk about foreign nations. Of all the nations of the world we are the one that combines the greatest amount of wealth with the smallest ability to defend that wealth. Surely one does not have to read history very much or ponder over philosophy a great deal in order to realize the truth that the one certain way to invite disaster is to be opulent, offensive, and unarmed. There is utter inconsistency between the ideal of making this nation the foremost commercial power in the world and of disarmament in the face of an armed world. There is utter inconsistency between the ideal of making this nation a power for international righteousness and at the same time refusing to make us a power efficient in anything save empty treaties and emptier promises.

I do not believe in a large standing army. Most emphatically I do not believe in militarism. Most emphatically I do not believe in any policy of aggression by us. But I do believe that no man is really fit to be the free citizen of a free republic unless he is able to bear arms and at need to serve with efficiency in the efficient army of the republic. This is no new thing with me. For years I have believed that the young men of the country should know how to use a rifle and should have a short period of military training which, while not taking them for any length of time from civil pursuits, would make them quickly capable of helping defend the country in case of need. When I was governor of New York, acting in conjunction with the administration at Washington under President McKinley, I secured the sending abroad of one of the best officers in the New York National Guard, Colonel William Cary Sanger, to study the Swiss system. As President I had to devote my attention chiefly to getting the navy built up. But surely the sight of what has happened abroad ought to awaken our people to the need of action, not only as regards our navy but as regards our land forces also.

Australia has done well in this respect. But Switzerland has worked out a comprehensive scheme with practical intelligence. She has not only solved the question of having men ready to fight, but she has solved the question of having arms to give these men. At present England is in more difficulty about arms than about men, and some of her people when sent to the front were armed with hunting rifles. Our own shortcomings are far greater. Indeed, they are so lamentable that it is hard to believe that our citizens as a whole know them. To equip half the number of men whom even the British now have in the field would tax our factories to the limit. In Switzerland, during the last two or three years of what corresponds to our high-school work the boy is thoroughly grounded in the rudiments of military training, discipline, and marksmanship. When he graduates he is put for some four to six months in the army to receive exactly the training he would get in time of war. After that he serves eight days a year and in addition often joins with his fellows in practising at a mark. He keeps his rifle and accoutrements in his home and is responsible for their condition. Efficiency is the watchword of Switzerland, and not least in its army. At the outbreak of this terrible war Switzerland was able to mobilize her forces in the corner of her territory between France and Germany as quickly as either of the great combatants could theirs; and no one trespassed upon her soil.

The Swiss training does not to any appreciable extent take the man away from his work. But it does make him markedly more efficient for his work. The training he gets and his short service with the colors render him appreciably better able to do whatever his job in life is, and, in addition, benefit his health and spirits. The service is a holiday, and a holiday of the best because of the most useful type.

There is no reason whatever why Americans should be unwilling or unable to do what Switzerland has done. We are a far wealthier country than Switzerland and could afford without the slightest strain the very trifling expense and the trifling consumption of time rendered necessary by such a system. It has really nothing in common with the universal service in the great conscript armies of the military powers. No man would be really taken out of industry. On the contrary, the average man would probably be actually benefited so far as doing his life-work is concerned. The system would be thoroughly democratic in its workings. No man would be exempted from the work and all would have to perform the work alike. It would be entirely possible to arrange that there should be a certain latitude as to the exact year when the four or six months' service was given.

Officers, of course, would need a longer training than the men. This could readily be furnished either by allowing numbers of extra students to take partial or short-term courses at West Point or by specifying optional courses in the high schools, the graduates of these special courses being tested carefully in their field-work and being required to give extra periods of service and being under the rigid supervision of the regular army. There could also be opportunities for promotion from the ranks for any one who chose to take the time and the trouble to fit himself.

The four or six months' service with the colors would be for the most part in the open field. The drill hall and the parade-ground do not teach more than five per cent of what a soldier must actually know. Any man who has had any experience with ordinary organizations of the National Guard when taken into camp knows that at first only a very limited number of the men have any idea of taking care of themselves and that the great majority suffer much from dyspepsia, just because they do not know how to take care of themselves. The soldier needs to spend some months in actual campaign practice under canvas with competent instructors before he gets to know his duty. If, however, he has had previous training in the schools of such a type as that given in Switzerland and then has this actual practice, he remains for some years efficient with no more training than eight or ten days a year.

The training must be given in large bodies. It is essential that men shall get accustomed to the policing and sanitary care of camps in which there are masses of soldiers. Moreover, officers and especially the higher officers are wholly useless in war time unless they are accustomed to handle masses of men in cooperation with one another.

There are small sections of our population out of which it is possible to improvise soldiers in a short time. Men who are accustomed to ride and to shoot and to live in the open and who are hardy and enduring and by nature possess the fighting edge already know most of what it is necessary that an infantryman or cavalryman should know, and they can be taught the remainder in a very short time by good officers. Morgan's Virginia Riflemen, Andrew Jackson's Tennesseans, Forrest's Southwestern Cavalry were all men of this kind; but even such men are of real use only after considerable training or else if their leaders are born fighters and masters of men. Such leaders are rare. The ordinary dweller in civilization has to be taught to shoot, to walk (or ride if he is in the cavalry), to cook for himself, to make himself comfortable in the open, and to take care of his feet and his health generally. Artillerymen and engineers need long special training.

It may well be that the Swiss on an average can be made into good troops quicker than our own men; but most assuredly there would be numbers of Americans who would not be behind the Swiss in such a matter. A body of volunteers of the kind I am describing would of course not be as good as a body of regulars of the same size, but they would be immeasurably better than the average soldiers produced by any system we now have or ever have had in connection with our militia. Our regular army would be strengthened by them at the very beginning and would be set free in its entirety for immediate aggressive action; and in addition a levy in mass of the young men of the right age would mean that two or three million troops were put into the field, who, although not as good as regulars, would at once be available in numbers sufficient to overwhelm any expeditionary force which it would be possible for any military power to send to our shores. The existence of such a force would render the immediate taking of cities like San Francisco, New York, or Boston an impossibility and would free us from all danger from sudden raids and make it impossible even for an army-corps to land with any prospect of success.

Our people are so entirely unused to things military that it is probably difficult for the average man to get any clear idea of our shortcomings. Unlike what is true in the military nations of the Old World, here the ordinary citizen takes no interest in the working of our War Department in time of peace. No President gains the slightest credit for himself by paying attention to it. Then when a crisis comes and the War Department breaks down, instead of the people accepting what has happened with humility as due to their own fault during the previous two or three decades, there is a roar of wrath against the unfortunate man who happens to be in office at the time. There was such a roar of wrath against Secretary Alger in the Spanish War. Now, as a matter of fact, ninety per cent of our shortcomings when the war broke out with Spain could not have been remedied by any action on the part of the Secretary of War. They were due to what had been done ever since the close of the Civil War.

We were utterly unprepared. There had been no real manœuvring of so much as a brigade and very rarely had any of our generals commanded even a good-sized regiment in the field. The enlisted men and the junior officers of the regular army were good. Most of the officers above the rank of captain were nearly worthless. There were striking exceptions of course, but, taking the average, I really believe that it would have been on the whole to the advantage of our army in 1898 if all the regular officers above the rank of captain had been retired and if all the captains who were unfit to be placed in the higher positions had also been retired. The lieutenants were good. The lack of administrative skill was even more marked than the lack of military skill. No one who saw the congestion of trains, supplies, animals, and men at Tampa will ever forget the impression of helpless confusion that it gave him. The volunteer forces included some organizations and multitudes of individuals offering first-class material. But, as a whole, the volunteer army would have been utterly helpless against any efficient regular force at the outset of the 1898 war, probably almost as inefficient as were the two armies which fought one another at Bull Run in 1861. Even the efficiency of the regular army itself was such merely by comparison with the volunteers. I do not believe that any army in the world offered finer material than was offered by the junior officers and enlisted men of the regular army which disembarked on Cuban soil in June, 1898; and by the end of the next two weeks probably the average individual infantry or cavalry organization therein was at least as good as the average organization of the same size in an Old-World army. But taking the army as a whole and considering its management from the time it began to assemble at Tampa until the surrender of Santiago, I seriously doubt if it was as efficient as a really good European or Japanese army of half the size. Since then we have made considerable progress. Our little army of occupation that went to Cuba at the time of the revolution in Cuba ten years ago was thoroughly well handled and did at least as well as any foreign force of the same size could have done. But it did not include ten thousand men, that is, it did not include as many men as the smallest military power in Europe would assemble any day for manœuvres.

This is no new thing in our history. If only we were willing to learn from our defeats and failures instead of paying heed purely to our successes, we would realize that what I have above described is one of the common phases of our history. In the War of 1812, at the outset of the struggle, American forces were repeatedly beaten, as at Niagara and Bladensburg, by an enemy one half or one quarter the strength of the American army engaged. Yet two years later these same American troops on the northern frontier, when trained and commanded by

Brown, Scott, and Ripley, proved able to do what the finest troops of Napoleon were unable to do, that is, meet the British regulars on equal terms in the open; and the Tennessee backwoodsmen and Louisiana volunteers, when mastered and controlled by the iron will and warlike genius of Andrew Jackson, performed at New Orleans a really great feat. During the year 1812 the American soldiers on shore suffered shameful and discreditable defeats, and yet their own brothers at sea won equally striking victories, and this because the men on shore were utterly unprepared and because the men at sea had been thoroughly trained and drilled long in advance.

Exactly the same lessons are taught by the histories of other nations. When, during the Napoleonic wars, a small force of veteran French soldiers landed in Ireland they defeated without an effort five times their number of British and Irish troops at Castlebar. Yet the men whom they thus drove in wild flight were the own brothers of and often the very same men who a few years later, under Wellington, proved an overmatch for the flower of the French forces. The nation that waits until the crisis is upon it before taking measures for its own safety pays heavy toll in the blood of its best and its bravest and in bitter shame and humiliation. Small is the comfort it can then take from the memory of the times when the noisy and feeble folk in its own ranks cried "Peace, peace," without taking one practical step to secure peace.

We can never follow out a worthy national policy, we can never be of benefit to others or to ourselves, unless we keep steadily in view as our ideal that of the just man armed, the man who is fearless, self-reliant, ready, because he has prepared himself for possible contingencies; the man who is scornful alike of those who would advise him to do wrong and of those who would advise him tamely to suffer wrong. The great war now being waged in Europe and the fact that no neutral nation has ventured to make even the smallest effort to alleviate[1] or even to

---

1   The much advertised sending of food and supplies to Belgium has been of most benefit to the German conquerors of Belgium. They have taken the money and food of the Belgians and permitted the Belgians to be supported by outsiders. Of course, it was far better to send them food, even under such conditions, than to let them starve; but the professional pacificists would do well to ponder the fact that if the neutral nations had been willing

protest against the wrongs that have been done show with lamentable clearness that all the peace congresses of the past fifteen years have accomplished precisely and exactly nothing so far as any great crisis is concerned. Fundamentally this is because they have confined themselves to mere words, seemingly without realizing that mere words are utterly useless unless translated into deeds and that an ounce of promise which is accompanied by provision for a similar ounce of effective performance is worth at least a ton of promise as to which no effective method of performance is provided. Furthermore, a very serious blunder has been to treat peace as the end instead of righteousness as the end. The greatest soldier-patriots of history, Timoleon, John Hamden, Andreas Hofer, Koerner, the great patriot-statesman-soldiers like Washington, the great patriot-statesmen like Lincoln whose achievements for good depended upon the use of soldiers, have all achieved their immortal claim to the gratitude of mankind by they did in just war. To condemn war in terms which include the wars these men waged or took part in precisely as they include the most wicked and unjust wars of history is to serve the devil and not God.

Again, these peace people have persistently and resolutely blinked facts. One of the peace congresses sat in New York at the very time that the feeling in California about the Japanese question gravely threatened the good relations between ourselves and the great empire of Japan. The only thing which at the moment could practically be done for the cause of peace was to secure some proper solution of the question at issue between ourselves and Japan. But this represented real effort, real thought. The peace congress paid not the slightest serious attention to the matter and instead devoted itself to listening to speeches which favored the abolition of the United States navy and even in one case the prohibiting the use of tin soldiers in nurseries because of the militaristic effect on the minds of the little boys and girls who played with them!

---

to prevent the invasion of Belgium, which could only be done by willingness and ability to use force, they would by this act of "war" have prevented more misery and suffering to innocent men, women, and children than the organized charity of all the "peaceful" nations of the world can now remove.

Ex-President Taft has recently said that it is hysterical to endeavor to prepare against war; and he at the same time explained that the only real possibility of war was to be found "in the wanton, reckless, wicked willingness on the part of a narrow section of the country to gratify racial prejudice and class hatred by flagrant breach of treaty right in the form of state law." This characterization is, of course, aimed at the State of California for its action toward the Japanese. If – which may Heaven forfend – any trouble comes because of the action of California toward the Japanese, a prime factor in producing it will be the treaty negotiated four years ago with Japan; and no clearer illustration can be given of the mischief that comes to our people from the habit our public men have contracted of getting cheap applause for themselves by making treaties which they know to be shams, which they know cannot be observed. The result of such action is that there is one set of real facts, those that actually exist and must be reckoned with, and another set of make-believe facts which do not exist except on pieces of paper or in after-dinner speeches, which are known to be false but which serve to deceive well-meaning pacificists. Four years ago there was in existence a long-standing treaty with Japan under which we reserved the right to keep out Japanese laborers. Every man of any knowledge whatever of conditions on the Pacific Slope, and, indeed, generally throughout this country, knew, and knows now, that any immigration in mass to this country of the Japanese, whether the immigrants be industrial laborers or men whose labor takes the form of agricultural work or even the form of small shopkeeping, was and is absolutely certain to produce trouble of the most dangerous kind. The then administration entered on a course of conduct as regards Manchuria which not only deeply offended the Japanese but actually achieved the result of uniting the Russians and Japanese against us. To make amends for this serious blunder the administration committed the far worse blunder of endeavoring to placate Japanese opinion by the negotiation of a new treaty in which our right to exclude Japanese laborers, that is, to prevent Japanese immigration in mass, was abandoned. The extraordinary and lamentable fact in the matter was that the California senators acquiesced in the treaty. Apparently they took the view, which so many of our public men do take and which they are encouraged to take by the unwisdom of those who demand impossible treaties, that they were perfectly willing to please some people by passing the treaty because, if necessary, the opponents of the treaty could at any time be placated by its violation. One item in securing their support was the statement by the then administration that the Japanese authorities had said that they would promise under a "gentlemen's agreement" to keep the immigrants out if only they were by treaty given the right to let them in. Under the preceding treaty, during my administration, the Japanese government had made and had in good faith kept such an agreement, the agreement being that as long as the Japanese government itself kept out Japanese immigrants and thereby relieved us of the necessity of passing any law to exclude them, no such law would be passed. Apparently the next administration did not perceive the fathomless difference between retaining the power to enact a law which was not enacted as long as no necessity for enacting it arose, and abandoning the power, surrendering the right, and trusting that the necessity to exercise it would not arise.

I immensely admire and respect the Japanese people. I prize their good-will. I am proud of my personal relations with some of their leading men. Fifty years ago there was no possible community between the Japanese and ourselves. The events of the last fifty years have been so extraordinary that now Japanese statesmen, generals, artists, writers, scientific men, business men, can meet our corresponding men on terms of entire equality. I am fortunate enough to have a number of Japanese friends. I value their friendship. They and I meet on a footing of absolute equality, socially, politically, and in every other way. I respect and regard them precisely as in the case of my German and Russian, French and English friends. But there is no use blinking the truth because it is unpleasant. As yet the differences between the Japanese who work with their hands and the Americans who work with their hands are such that it is absolutely impossible for them, when brought into contact with one another in great numbers, to get on. Japan would not permit any immigration in mass of our people into her territory, and it is wholly inadvisable that there should be such immigration of her people into our territory. This is not because either side is inferior to the other but because they are different. As a matter of fact, these differences are sometimes in favor of the Japanese and sometimes in favor of the Americans. But they are so marked that at this time, whatever may be the case in the future, friction and trouble are certain to come if there is any immigration in mass of Japanese into this country, exactly as friction and trouble have actually come in British Columbia from this cause, and have been prevented from coming in Australia only by the most rigid exclusion laws. Under these conditions the way to avoid trouble is not by making believe that things which are not so are so but by courteously and firmly facing the situation. The two nations should be given absolutely reciprocal treatment. Students, statesmen, publicists, scientific men, all travellers, whether for business or pleasure, and all men engaged in international business, whether Japanese or American, should have absolute right of entry into one another's countries and should be treated with the highest consideration while therein, but no settlement in mass should be permitted of the people of either country in the other country. All travelling and sojourning by the people of either country in the other country should be encouraged, but there should be no immigration of workers to, no settlement in, either country by the people of the other. I advocate this solution, which for years I have advocated, because I am not merely a friend but an intense admirer of Japan, because I am most anxious that America should learn from Japan the great amount that Japan can teach us and because I wish to work for the best possible feeling between the two countries. Each country has interests in the Pacific which can best be served by their cordial co-operation on a footing of frank and friendly equality; and in eastern Asiatic waters the interest and therefore the proper dominance of Japan are and will be greater than those of any other nation. If such a plan as that above advocated were once adopted by both our nations all sources of friction between the two countries would vanish at once. Ultimately I have no question that all restrictions of movement from one country to the other could be dispensed with. But to attempt to dispense with them in our day and our generation will fail; and even worse failure will attend the attempt to make believe to dispense with them while not doing so.

It is eminently necessary that the United States should in good faith observe its treaties, and it is therefore eminently necessary not to pass treaties which it is absolutely certain will not be obeyed, and which themselves provoke disobedience to them. The height of folly, of course, is to pass treaties which will not be obeyed and the disregard of which may cause the gravest possible trouble, even war, and at the same time to refuse to prepare for war and to pass other foolish treaties calculated to lure our people into the belief that there will never be war.

I advocate that our preparedness take such shape as to fit us to resist aggression, not to encourage us in aggression. I advocate preparedness that will enable us to defend our own shores and to defend the Panama Canal and Hawaii and Alaska, and prevent the seizure of territory at the expense of any commonwealth of the western hemisphere by any military power of the Old World. I advocate this being done in the most democratic manner possible. We Americans do not realize how fundamentally democratic our army really is. When I served in Cuba it was under General Sam Young and alongside of General Adna Chaffee. Both had entered the American army as enlisted men in the Civil War. Later, as President, I made both of them in succession lieutenant-generals and commanders of the army. On the occasion when General Chaffee was to appear at the White House for the first time as lieutenant-general, General Young sent him his own starred shoulder-straps with a little note saying that they were from "Private Young, '61, to Private Chaffee, '61." Both of the fine old fellows represented the best type of citizen-soldier. Each was simply and sincerely devoted to peace and justice. Each was incapable of advocating our doing wrong to others. Neither could have understood willingness on the part of any American to see the United States submit tamely to insult or injury. Both typified the attitude that we Americans should take in our dealings with foreign countries.

Chapter IX

Our Peacemaker, the Navy

The course of the present administration in foreign affairs has now and then combined officiously offensive action toward foreign powers with tame submission to wrong-doing by foreign powers. As a nation we have refused to do our duty to others and yet we have at times tamely submitted to wrong at the hands of others. This has been notably true of our conduct in Mexico; and we have come perilously near such conduct in the case of Japan. It is also true of our activities as regards the European war. We failed to act in accordance with our obligations as a signatory power to the Hague treaties. In addition to the capital crime committed against Belgium we have seen outrage after outrage perpetrated in violation of the Hague conventions, and yet the administration has never ventured so much as a protest. It has even at times, and with wavering and vacillation, adopted policies unjust to one or the other of the two sets of combatants. But it has immediately abandoned these policies when the combatants in violent and improper fashion overrode them; and it has submitted with such tame servility to whatever the warring nations have dictated that in effect we see, as Theodore Woolsey, the expert on international law, has pointed out, the American government protecting belligerent interests abroad at the expense of neutral interests both at home and abroad. Not since the Napoleonic wars have belligerents acted with such high-handed disregard of the rights of neutrals. Germany was the first and greatest offender; and when we failed to protest in her case the administration perhaps felt ashamed to protest, felt that it was estopped from protesting, in other cases. England in its turn has violated our neutrality rights, and while exercising both force and ingenuity in making this violation effective has protested as if she herself were the injured party. As a matter of fact, England and France should note that in view of their command of the seas our war trade is of such value to them that certain congressmen, whose interest in Germany surpasses their interest in the United States, have sought by law totally to prohibit it. This proposed – and thoroughly improper – action is a sufficient answer to the charges of the Allies, and should remind them how ill they requite the service rendered by our merchants when they seek to block all our intercourse with other nations. They, however, are only to be blamed for short-sightedness; there is no reason why they should pay heed to American interests. But the administration should represent American interests; it should see that while we perform our duties as neutrals we should be protected in our rights as neutrals; and one of these rights is the trade in contraband. To prohibit this is to take part in the war for the benefit of one belligerent at the expense of another and to our own cost.

Of course it would be an ignoble action on our part after having conspicuously failed to protest against the violation of Belgian neutrality to show ourselves overeager to protest against comparatively insignificant violations of our own neutral rights. But we should never have put ourselves in such a position as to make insistence on our own rights seem disregard for the rights of others. The proper course for us to pursue was, on the one hand, scrupulously to see that we did not so act as to injure any contending nation, unless required to do so in the name of morality and of our solemn treaty obligations, and also fearlessly to act on behalf of other nations which were wronged, as required by these treaty obligations; and, on the other hand, with courteous firmness to warn any nation which, for instance, seized or searched our ships against the accepted rules of international conduct that this we could not permit and that such a course should not be persevered in by any nation which desired our good-will. I believe I speak for at least a considerable portion of our people when I say that we wish to make it evident that we feel sincere goodwill toward all nations; that any action we take against any nation is taken with the greatest reluctance and only because the wrong-doing of that nation imposes a distinct, although painful, duty upon us; and yet that we do not intend ourselves to submit to wrong-doing from any nation.

Until an efficient world league for peace is in more than mere process of formation the United States must depend upon itself for protection where its vital interests are concerned. All the youth of the nation should be trained in warlike exercises and in the use of arms – as well as in the indispensable virtues of courage, self-restraint, and endurance – so as to be fit for national defense. But the right arm of the nation must be its navy. Our navy is our most efficient peacemaker. In order to use the navy effectively we should clearly define to ourselves the policy we intend to follow and the limits over which we expect our power to extend. Our own coasts, Alaska, Hawaii, and the Panama Canal and its approaches should represent the sphere in which we should expect to be able, single-handed, to meet and master any opponent from overseas.

I exclude the Philippines. This is because I feel that the present administration has definitely committed us to a course of action which will make the early and complete severance of the Philippines from us not merely desirable but necessary. I have never felt that the Philippines were of any special use to us. But I have felt that we had a great task to perform there and that a great nation is benefited by doing a great task. It was our bounden duty to work primarily for the interests of the Filipinos; but it was also our bounden duty, inasmuch as the entire responsibility lay upon us, to consult our own judgment and not theirs in finally deciding what was to be done. It was our duty to govern the islands or to get out of the islands. It was most certainly not our duty to take the responsibility of staying in the islands without governing them. Still less was it – or is it – our duty to enter into joint arrangements with other powers about the islands; arrangements of confused responsibility and divided power of the kind sure to cause mischief. I had hoped that we would continue to govern the islands until we were certain that they were able to govern themselves in such fashion as to do justice to other nations and to repel injustice committed on them by other nations. To substitute for such government by ourselves either a government by the Filipinos with us guaranteeing them against outsiders, or a joint guarantee between us and outsiders, would be folly. It is eminently desirable to guarantee the neutrality of small civilized nations which have a high social and cultural status and which are so advanced that they do not fall into disorder or commit wrong-doing on others. But it is eminently undesirable to guarantee the neutrality or sovereignty of an inherently weak nation which is impotent to preserve order at home, to repel assaults from abroad, or to refrain from doing wrong to outsiders. It is even more undesirable to give such a guarantee with no intention of making it really effective. That this is precisely what the present administration would be delighted to do has been shown by its refusal to live up to its Hague promises at the very time that it was making similar new international promises by the batch. To enter into a joint guarantee of neutrality which in emergencies can only be rendered effective by force of arms is to incur a serious responsibility which ought to be undertaken in a serious spirit. To enter into it with no intention of using force, or of preparing force, in order at need to make it effective, represents the kind of silliness which is worse than wickedness.

Above all, we should keep our promises. The present administration was elected on the outright pledge of giving the Filipinos independence. Apparently its course in the Philippines has proceeded upon the theory that the Filipinos are now fit to govern themselves. Whatever may be our personal and individual beliefs in this matter, we ought not as a nation to break faith or even to seem to break faith. I hope therefore that the Filipinos will be given their independence at an early date and without any guarantee from us which might in any way hamper our future action or commit us to staying on the Asiatic coast. I do not believe we should keep any foothold whatever in the Philippines. Any kind of position by us in the Philippines merely results in making them our heel of Achilles if we are attacked by a foreign power. They can be of no compensating benefit to us. If we were to retain complete control over them and to continue the course of action which in the past sixteen years has resulted in such immeasurable benefit for them, then I should feel that it was our duty to stay and work for them in spite of the expense incurred by us and the risk we thereby ran. But inasmuch as we have now promised to leave them and as we are now abandoning our power to work efficiently for and in them, I do not feel that we are warranted in staying in the islands in an equivocal position, thereby incurring great risk to ourselves without conferring any real compensating advantage, of a kind which we are bound to take into account, on the Filipinos themselves. If the Filipinos are entitled to independence then we are entitled to be freed from all the responsibility and risk which our presence in the islands entails upon us.

The great nations of southernmost South America, Brazil, the Argentine, and Chile are now so far advanced in stability and power that there is no longer any need of applying the Monroe Doctrine as far as they are concerned; and this also relieves us as regards Uruguay and Paraguay the former of which is well advanced and neither of which has any interests with which we need particularly concern ourselves. As regards all these powers, therefore, we now have no duty save that doubtless if they got into difficulties and desired our aid we would gladly extend it, just as, for instance, we would to Australia and Canada. But we can now proceed on the assumption that they are able to help themselves and that any help we should be required to give would be given by us as an auxiliary rather than as a principal.

Our naval problem, therefore, is primarily to provide for the protection of our own coasts and for the protection and policing of Hawaii, Alaska, and the Panama Canal and its approaches. This offers a definite problem which should be solved by our naval men. It is for them, having in view the lessons taught by this war, to say what is the exact type of fleet we require, the number and kind of submarines, of destroyers, of mines, and of air-ships to be used against hostile fleets, in addition to the cruisers and great fighting craft which must remain the backbone of the navy. Civilians may be competent to pass on the merits of the plans suggested by the naval men, but it is the naval men themselves who must make and submit the plans in detail. Lay opinion, however, should keep certain elementary facts steadily in mind.

The navy must primarily be used for offensive purposes. Forts, not the navy, are to be used for defense. The only permanently efficient type of defensive is the offensive. A portion, and a very important portion, of our naval strength must be used with our own coast ordinarily as a base, its striking radius being only a few score miles, or a couple of hundred at the outside. The events of this war have shown that submarines can play a tremendous part. We should develop our force of submarines and train the officers and crews who have charge of them to the highest pitch of efficiency – for they will be useless in time of war unless those aboard them have been trained in time of peace. These submarines, when used in connection with destroyers and with air-ships, can undoubtedly serve to minimize the danger of successful attack on our own shores. But the prime lesson of the war, as regards the navy, is that the nation with a powerful seagoing navy, although it may suffer much annoyance and loss, yet is able on the whole to take the offensive and do great damage to a nation with a less powerful navy. Great Britain's naval superiority over Germany has enabled her completely to paralyze all Germany's sea commerce and to prevent goods from entering her ports. What is far more important, it has enabled the British to land two or three hundred thousand men to aid the French, and has enabled Canada and Australia to send a hundred thousand men from the opposite ends of the earth to Great Britain. If Germany had had the more powerful navy England would now have suffered the fate of Belgium.

The capital work done by the German cruisers in the Atlantic, the Pacific, and the Indian Oceans shows how much can be accomplished in the way of hurting and damaging an enemy by even the weaker power if it possesses fine ships, well handled, able to operate thousands of miles from their own base. We must not fail to recognize this. Neither must we fail heartily and fully to recognize the capital importance of submarines as well as air-ships, torpedo-boat destroyers, and mines, as proved by the events of the last three months. But nothing that has yet occurred warrants us in feeling that we can afford to ease up in our programme of building battle-ships and cruisers, especially the former. The German submarines have done wonderfully in this war; their cruisers have done gallantly. But so far as Great Britain is concerned the vital and essential feature has been the fact that her great battle fleet has kept the German fleet immured in its own home ports, has protected Britain from invasion, and has enabled her land strength to be used to its utmost capacity beside the armies of France and Belgium. If the men who for years have clamored against Britain's being prepared had had their way, if Britain during the last quarter of a century had failed to continue the up-building of her navy, if the English statesmen corresponding to President Wilson and Mr. Bryan had seen their ideas triumph, England would now be off the map as a great power and the

British Empire would have dissolved, while London, Liverpool, and Birmingham would be in the condition of Antwerp and Brussels.

The efficiency of the German personnel at sea has been no less remarkable than the efficiency of the German personnel on land. This is due partly to the spirit of the nation and partly to what is itself a consequence of that spirit, the careful training of the navy during peace under the conditions of actual service. When, early in 1909, our battle fleet returned from its sixteen months' voyage around the world there was no navy in the world which, size for size, ship for ship, and squadron for squadron, stood at a higher pitch of efficiency. We blind ourselves to the truth if we believe that the same is true now. During the last twenty months, ever since Secretary Meyer left the Navy Department, there has been in our navy a great falling off relatively to other nations. It was quite impossible to avoid this while our national affairs were handled as they have recently been handled. The President who intrusts the Departments of State and the Navy to gentlemen like Messrs. Bryan and Daniels deliberately invites disaster, in the event of serious complications with a formidable foreign opponent. On the whole, there is no class of our citizens, big or small, who so emphatically deserve well of the country as the officers and the enlisted men of the army and navy. No navy in the world has such fine stuff out of which to make man-of-war's men. But they must be heartily backed up, heartily supported, and sedulously trained. They must be treated well, and, above all, they must be treated so as to encourage the best among them by sharply discriminating against the worst. The utmost possible efficiency should he demanded of them. They are emphatically and in every sense of the word men; and real men resent with impatient contempt a policy under which less than their best is demanded. The finest material is utterly worthless without the best personnel. In such a highly specialized service as the navy constant training of a purely military type is an absolute necessity. At present our navy is lamentably short in many different material directions. There is actually but one torpedo for each torpedo tube. It seems incredible that such can be the case; yet it is the case. We are many thousands of men short in our enlistments. We are lamentably short in certain types of vessel. There is grave doubt as to the efficiency of many of our submarines and destroyers. But the shortcomings in our training are even more lamentable. To keep the navy cruising near Vera Cruz and in Mexican waters, without manœuvring, invites rapid deterioration. For nearly two years there has been no fleet manœuvring; and this fact by itself probably means a twenty-five per cent loss of efficiency. During the same periods most of the ships have not even had division gun practice. Not only should our navy be as large as our position and interest demand but it should be kept continually at the highest point of efficiency and should never be used save for its own appropriate military purposes. Of this elementary fact the present administration seems to be completely ignorant.

President Wilson and Secretary Daniels assert that our navy is in efficient shape. Admiral Fiske's testimony is conclusive to the contrary, although it was very cautiously given, as is but natural when a naval officer, if he tells the whole truth, must state what is unpleasant for his superiors to hear. Other naval officers have pointed out our deficiencies, and the newspapers state that some of them have been reprimanded for so doing. But there is no need for their testimony. There is one admitted fact which is absolutely conclusive in the matter. There has been no fleet manœuvring during the past twenty-two months. In spite of fleet manœuvring the navy may be unprepared. But it is an absolute certainty that without fleet manœuvring it cannot possibly be prepared. In the unimportant domain of sport there is not a man who goes to see the annual football game between Harvard and Yale who would not promptly cancel his ticket if either university should propose to put into the field a team which, no matter how good the players were individually, had not been practised as a team during the preceding sixty days. If in such event the president of either university or the coach of the team should announce that in spite of never having had any team practice the team was nevertheless in first-class condition, there is literally no intelligent follower of the game who would regard the utterance as serious. Why should President Wilson and Secretary Daniels expect the American public to show less intelligence as regards the vital matter of our navy than they do as regards a mere sport, a mere play? For twenty-two months there has been no fleet manœuvring. Since in the daily press, early in November, I,

with emphasis, called attention to this fact Mr. Daniels has announced that shortly manœuvring will take place; and of course the failure
to manœuvre for nearly two years has been due less to Mr. Daniels
than to President Wilson's futile and mischievous Mexican policy and
his entire ignorance of the needs of the navy. I am glad that the administration has tardily waked up to the necessity of taking some steps
to make the navy efficient, and if the President and the Secretary of
the Navy bring forth fruits meet for repentance, I will most heartily
acknowledge the fact – just as it has given me the utmost pleasure to
praise and support President Wilson's Secretary of War, Mr. Garrison.
But misstatements as to actual conditions make but a poor preparation for the work of remedying these conditions, and President Wilson and Secretary Daniels try to conceal from the people our ominous
naval shortcomings. The shortcomings are far-reaching, alike in material, organization, and practical training. The navy is absolutely unprepared; its efficiency has been terribly reduced under and because of
the action of President Wilson and Secretary Daniels. Let them realize
this fact and do all they can to remedy the wrong they have committed. Let Congress realize its own shortcomings. Far-reaching and tho-
roughgoing treatment, continued for a period of at least two and in all
probability three years, is needed if the navy is to be placed on an equality, unit for unit, no less than in the mass, with the navies of England,
Germany, and Japan. In the present war the deeds of the *Emden*, of the
German submarines, of Von Spee's squadron, have shown not merely
efficiency but heroism; and the navies of Great Britain and Japan have
been handled in masterly manner. Have the countrymen of Farragut,
of Cushing, Buchanan, Winslow, and Semmes, of Decatur, Hull, Perry,
and MacDonough, lost their address and courage, and are they willing
to sink below the standard set by their forefathers?

It has been said that the United States never learns by experience
but only by disaster. Such method of education may at times prove
costly. The slothful or short-sighted citizens who are now misled by
the cries of the ultrapacificists, would do well to remember events connected with the outbreak of the war with Spain. I was then Assistant
Secretary of the Navy. At one bound our people passed from a condition of smug confidence that war never could occur (a smug confi-

dence just as great as any we feel at present) to a condition of utterly unreasoning panic over what might be done to us by a very weak antagonist. One governor of a seaboard State announced that none of the National Guard regiments would be allowed to respond to the call of the President because they would be needed to prevent a Spanish invasion of that State – the Spaniards being about as likely to make such an invasion as we were to invade Timbuctoo or Turkestan. One congressman besought me to send a battle-ship to protect Jekyll Island, off the coast of Georgia. Another congressman asked me to send a battle-ship to protect a summer colony which centred around a large Atlantic-coast hotel in Connecticut. In my own neighborhood on Long Island clauses were gravely inserted into the leases of property to the effect that if the Spaniards destroyed the property the leases should terminate. Chambers of commerce, boards of trade, municipal authorities, leading business men, from one end of the country to the other, hysterically demanded, each of them, that a ship should be stationed to defend some particular locality; the theory being that our navy should be strung along both seacoasts, each ship by itself, in a purely defensive attitude – thereby making certain that even the Spanish navy could pick them all up in detail. One railway president came to protest to me against the choice of Tampa as a point of embarkation for our troops, on the ground that his railway was entitled to its share of the profit of transporting troops and munitions of war and that his railway went to New Orleans. The very senators and congressmen who had done everything in their power to prevent the building up and the efficient training of the navy screamed and shrieked loudest to have the navy diverted from its proper purpose and used to protect unimportant seaports. Surely our congressmen and, above all, our people need to learn that in time of crisis peace treaties are worthless, and the ultrapacifists of both sexes merely a burden on and a detriment to the country as a whole; that the only permanently useful defensive is the offensive, and that the navy is properly the offensive weapon of the nation.

The navy of the United States is the right arm of the United States and is emphatically the peacemaker. Woe to our country if we permit that right arm to become palsied or even to become flabby and inefficient!

Chapter X

Preparedness against War

Military preparedness meets two needs. In the first place, it is a partial insurance against war. In the next place, it is a partial guarantee that if war comes the country will certainly escape dishonor and will probably escape material loss.

The question of preparedness cannot be considered at all until we get certain things clearly in our minds. Right thinking, wholesome thinking, is essential as a preliminary to sound national action. Until our people understand the folly of certain of the arguments advanced against the action this nation needs, it is, of course, impossible to expect them to take such action.

The first thing to understand is the fact that preparedness for war does not always insure peace but that it very greatly increases the chances of securing peace. Foolish people point out nations which, in spite of preparedness for war, have seen war come upon them, and then exclaim that preparedness against war is of no use. Such an argument is precisely like saying that the existence of destructive fires in great cities shows that there is no use in having a fire department. A fire department, which means preparedness against fire, does not prevent occasional destructive fires, but it does greatly diminish and may completely minimize the chances for wholesale destruction by fire. Nations that are prepared for war occasionally suffer from it; but if they are unprepared for it they suffer far more often and far more radically.

Fifty years ago China, Korea, and Japan were in substantially the same stage of culture and civilization. Japan, whose statesmen had vision and whose people had the fighting edge, began a course of military preparedness, and the other two nations (one of them in natural resources immeasurably superior to Japan) remained unprepared. In consequence, Japan has immensely increased her power and standing and is wholly free from all danger of military invasion. Korea on the contrary, having first been dominated by Russia has now been conquered by Japan. China has been partially dismembered; one half of her territories are now subject to the dominion of foreign nations, which have time and again waged war between themselves on these territories, and her remaining territory is kept by her purely because these foreign nations are jealous of one another.

In 1870 France was overthrown and suffered by far the most damaging and disastrous defeat she had suffered since the days of Joan of Arc – because she was not prepared. In the present war she has suffered terribly, but she is beyond all comparison better off than she was in 1870, because she has been prepared. Poor Belgium, in spite of being prepared, was almost destroyed, because great neutral nations – the United States being the chief offender – have not yet reached the standard of international morality and of willingness to fight for righteousness which must be attained before they can guarantee small, well-behaved, civilized nations against cruel disaster. England, because she was prepared as far as her navy is concerned, has been able to avoid Belgium's fate; and, on the other hand, if she had been as prepared with her army as France, she would probably have been able to avert the war and, if this could not have been done, would at any rate have been able to save both France and Belgium from invasion.

In recent years Rumania, Bulgaria, and Serbia have at times suffered terribly, and in some cases have suffered disaster, in spite of being prepared for war; but Bosnia and Herzegovina are under alien rule at this moment because they could no more protect themselves against Austria than they could against Turkey. While Greece was unprepared she was able to accomplish nothing, and she encountered disaster. As soon as she was prepared, she benefited immensely.

Switzerland, at the time of the Napoleonic wars, was wholly unprepared for war. In spite of her mountains, her neighbors overran her at will. Great battles were fought on her soil, including one great battle between the French and the Russians; but the Swiss took no part in these battles. Their territory was practically annexed to the French Republic, and they were domineered over first by the Emperor Napoleon and then by his enemies. It was a bitter lesson, but the Swiss learned it. Since then they have gradually prepared for war as no other small state of Europe has done, and it is in consequence of this preparedness that none of the combatants has violated Swiss territory in the present struggle.

The briefest examination of the facts shows that unpreparedness for war tends to lead to immeasurable disaster, and that preparedness, while it does not certainly avert war any more than the fire department of a city certainly averts fire, yet tends very strongly to guarantee the nation against war and to secure success in war if it should unhappily arise.

Another argument advanced against preparedness for war is that such preparedness incites war. This, again, is not in accordance with the facts. Unquestionably certain nations have at times prepared for war with a view to foreign conquest. But the rule has been that unpreparedness for war does not have any real effect in securing peace, although it is always apt to make war disastrous, and that preparedness for war generally goes hand in hand with an increased caution in going to war.

Striking examples of these truths are furnished by the history of the Spanish-American states. For nearly three quarters of a century after these states won their independence their history was little else than a succession of bloody revolutions and of wars among themselves as well as with outsiders, while during the same period there was little or nothing done in the way of effective military preparedness by one of them. During the last twenty or thirty years, however, certain of them, notably Argentina and Chile, have prospered and become stable. Their stability has been partly caused by, and partly accompanied by, a great increase in military preparedness. During this period Argentina and Chile have known peace as they never knew it before, and as the other Spanish-American countries have not known it either before or since, and at the same time their military efficiency has enormously increased.

Proportionately, Argentina and Chile are in military strength beyond all comparison more efficient than the United States; and if our navy is permitted to deteriorate as it has been deteriorating for nearly two years, the same statement can soon be made, although with more qualification, of their naval strength. Preparedness for war has made them far less liable to have war. It has made them less and not more aggressive. It has also made them for the first time efficient potential factors in maintaining the Monroe Doctrine as coguarantors, on a footing of complete equality with the United States. The Monroe Doctrine, conceived not merely as a measure of foreign policy vital to the welfare of the United States, but even more as the proper joint foreign policy of all American nations, is by far the most efficient guarantee against war that can be offered the western hemisphere. By whatever name it is called, it is absolutely indispensable in order to keep this hemisphere mistress of its own destinies, able to prevent any part of it from falling under the dominion of any Old World power, and able absolutely to control in its own interest all colonization on and immigration to our shores from either Europe or Asia.

The bloodiest and most destructive war in Spanish-American history, that waged by Brazil, Argentina, and Uruguay against Paraguay, was waged when all the nations were entirely unprepared for war, especially the three victorious nations. During the last two or three decades Mexico, the Central American states, Colombia, and Venezuela have been entirely unprepared for war, as compared with Chile and Argentina. Yet, whereas Chile and Argentina have been at peace, the other states mentioned have been engaged in war after war of the most bloody and destructive character. Entire lack of preparedness for war has gone hand in hand with war of the worst type and with all the worst sufferings that war can bring.

The lessons taught by Spanish-America are paralleled elsewhere. When Greece was entirely unprepared for war she nevertheless went to war with Turkey, exactly as she did when she was prepared; the only difference was that in the one case she suffered disaster and in the other she did not. The war between Italy and Turkey was due wholly to the fact that Turkey was not prepared – that she had no navy. The fact that in 1848 Prussia was entirely unprepared, and moreover had just been engaged in a revolution heartily approved by all the ultra-pacificists and professional humanitarians, did not prevent her from entering on a war with Denmark. It merely prevented the war from being successful.

Utter and complete lack of preparation on our part did not prevent our entering into war with Great Britain in 1812 and with Mexico in 1848. It merely exposed us to humiliation and disaster in the former war; in the latter, Mexico was even worse off as regards preparation than we were. As for civil war, of course military unpreparedness has not only never prevented it but, on the contrary, seems usually to have been one of the inciting causes.

The fact that unpreparedness does not mean peace ought to be patent to every American who will think of what has occurred in this country during the last seventeen years. In 1898 we were entirely unprepared for war. No big nation, save and except our opponent, Spain, was more utterly unprepared than we were at that time, nor more utterly unfit for military operations. This did not, however, mean that peace was secured for a single additional hour. Our army and navy had been neglected for thirty-three years. This was due largely to the attitude of the spiritual forebears of those eminent clergymen, earnest social workers, and professionally humanitarian and peace-loving editors, publicists, writers for syndicates, speakers for peace congresses, pacificist college presidents, and the like who have recently come forward to protest against any inquiry into the military condition of this nation, on the ground that to supply our ships and forts with sufficient ammunition and to fill up the depleted ranks of the army and navy, and in other ways to prepare against war, will tend to interfere with peace. In 1898 the gentlemen of this sort had had their way for thirty-three years. Our army and navy had been grossly neglected. But the unpreparedness due to this neglect had not the slightest effect of any kind in preventing the war. The only effect it had was to cause the unnecessary and useless loss of thousands of lives in the war. Hundreds of young men perished in the Philippine trenches because, while the soldiers of Aguinaldo had modern rifles with smokeless powder, our troops had only the old black-powder Springfield. Hundreds more, nay thousands, died or had their health impaired for life in fever camps here in our own country and in the Philippines and Cuba, and suffered on transports, because we were entirely unprepared for war, and therefore no one knew how to take care of our men. The lives of these brave young volunteers were the price that this country paid for the past action of men like the clergyman, college presidents, editors, and humanitarians in question – none of whom, by the way, risked their own lives. They were also the price that this country paid for having had in previous cabinets just such incompetents as in time of peace Presidents so often, for political reasons, put into American cabinets – just such incompetents as President Wilson has put into the Departments of State and of the Navy.

Now and then the ultrapacificists point out the fact that war is bad because the best men go to the front and the worst stay at home. There is a certain truth in this. I do not believe that we ought to permit pacificists to stay at home and escape all risk, while their braver and more patriotic fellow countrymen fight for the national well-being. It is for this reason that I wish that we would provide for universal military training for our young men, and in the event of serious war make all men do their part instead of letting the whole burden fall upon the gallant souls who volunteer. But as there is small likelihood of any such course being followed in the immediate future, I at least hope that we will so prepare ourselves in time of peace as to make our navy and army thoroughly efficient; and also to enable us in time of war to handle our volunteers in such shape that the loss among them shall be due to the enemy's bullets instead of, as is now the case, predominantly to preventable sickness which we do not prevent. I call the attention of the ultrapacificists to the fact that in the last half century all the losses among our men caused by "militarism," as they call it, that is, by the arms of an enemy in consequence of our going to war, have been far less than the loss caused among these same soldiers by applied pacifism, that is, by our government having yielded to the wishes of the pacificists and declined in advance to make any preparations for war. The professional peace people have benefited the foes and ill-wishers of their country; but it is probably the literal fact to say that in the actual deed, by the obstacles they have thrown in the way of making adequate preparation in advance, they have caused more loss of life among American soldiers, fighting for the honor of the American flag, during the fifty years since the close of the Civil War than has been caused by the foes whom we have fought during that period.[2]

2   Some oft the leading pacificists are men who have made great fortunes in industry. Of course industry inevitably takes toll of life. Far more lives have been lost in this country by men engaged in bridge building, tunnel digging, mining, steel manufacturing, the erection

But the most striking instance of the utter failure of unpreparedness to stop war has been shown by President Wilson himself. President Wilson has made himself the great official champion of unpreparedness in military and naval matters. His words and his actions about foreign war have their nearest parallel in the words and the actions of President Buchanan about civil war; and in each case there has been the same use of verbal adroitness to cover mental hesitancy. By his words and his actions President Wilson has done everything possible to prevent this nation from making its army and navy effective and to increase the inefficiency which he already found existing. We were unprepared when he took office, and every month since we have grown still less prepared. Yet this fact did not prevent President Wilson, the great apostle of unpreparedness, the great apostle of pacificism and anti-militarism, from going to war with Mexico last spring. It merely prevented him, or, to speak more accurately, the same mental peculiarities which made him the apostle of unpreparedness also prevented him, from making the war efficient. His conduct rendered the United States an object of international derision because of the way in which its affairs were managed. President Wilson made no declaration of war. He did not in any way satisfy the requirements of common international law before acting. He invaded a neighboring state, with which he himself insisted we were entirely at peace, and occupied the most considerable seaport of the country after military operations which resulted in the loss of the lives of perhaps twenty of our men and five or ten times that number of Mexicans; and then he sat supine, and refused to allow either the United States or Mexico to reap any benefit from what had been done.

It is idle to say that such an amazing action was not war. It was an utterly futile war and achieved nothing; but it was war. We had ample justification for interfering in Mexico and even for going to war with

---

of sky-scrapers, the operations of the fishing fleet, and the like, than in all our battles in all our foreign wars put together. Such loss of life no more justifies us in opposing righteous wars than in opposing necessary industry. There was certainly far greater loss of life, in the industries out of which Mr. Carnegie made his gigantic fortune than has occured among our troops in war during the time covered by Mr. Carnegie's activities on behalf of peace.

Mexico, if after careful consideration this course was deemed necessary. But the President did not even take notice of any of the atrocious wrongs Americans had suffered, or deal with any of the grave provocations we had received. His statement of justification was merely that "we are in Mexico to serve mankind, if we can find a way." Evidently he did not have in his mind any particular idea of how he was to "serve mankind," for, after staying eight months in Mexico, he decided that he could not "find a way" and brought his army home. He had not accomplished one single thing. At one time it was said that we went to Vera Cruz to stop the shipment of arms into Mexico. But after we got there we allowed the shipments to continue. At another time it was said that we went there in order to exact an apology for an insult to the flag. But we never did exact the apology, and we left Vera Cruz without taking any steps to get an apology. In all our history there has been no more extraordinary example of queer infirmity of purpose in an important crisis than was shown by President Wilson in this matter. His business was either not to interfere at all or to interfere hard and effectively. This was the sole policy which should have been allowed by regard for the dignity and honor of the government of the United States and the welfare of our people. In the actual event President Wilson interfered, not enough to quell civil war, not enough to put a stop to or punish the outrages on American citizens, but enough to incur fearful responsibilities. Then, having without authority of any kind, either under the Constitution or in international law or in any other way, thus interfered, and having interfered to worse than no purpose, and having made himself and the nation partly responsible for the atrocious wrongs committed on Americans and on foreigners generally in Mexico by the bandit chiefs whom he was more or less furtively supporting, President Wilson abandoned his whole policy and drew out of Mexico to resume his "watchful waiting." When the President, who has made himself the chief official exponent of the doctrine of unpreparedness, thus shows that even in his hands unpreparedness has not the smallest effect in preventing war, there ought to be little need of discussing the matter further.

Preparedness for war occasionally has a slight effect in creating or increasing an aggressive and militaristic spirit. Far more often it distinctly diminishes it. In Switzerland, for instance, which we can well afford to take as a model for ourselves, effectiveness in preparation, and the retention and development of all the personal qualities which give the individual man the fighting edge, have in no shape or way increased the militarist or aggressive spirit. On the contrary, they have doubtless been among the factors that have made the Swiss so much more law-abiding and less homicidal than we are.

The ultrapacificists have been fond of prophesying the immediate approach of a universally peaceful condition throughout the world, which will render it unnecessary to prepare against war because there will be no more war. This represents in some cases well-meaning and pathetic folly. In other cases it represents mischievous and inexcusable folly. But it always represents folly. At best, it represents the inability of some well-meaning men of weak mind, and of some men of strong but twisted mind, either to face or to understand facts.

These prophets of the inane are not peculiar to our own day. A little over a century and a quarter ago a noted Italian pacificist and philosopher, Aurelio Bertela, summed up the future of civilized mankind as follows: "The political system of Europe has arrived at perfection. An equilibrium has been attained which henceforth will preserve peoples from subjugation. Few reforms are now needed and these will be accomplished peaceably. Europe has no need to fear revolution."

These sapient statements (which have been paralleled by hundreds of utterances in the many peace congresses of the last couple of decades) were delivered in 1787, the year in which the French Assembly of Notables ushered in the greatest era of revolution, domestic turmoil, and international war in all history – an era which still continues and which shows not the smallest sign of coming to an end. Never before have there been wars on so great a scale as during this century and a quarter; and the greatest of all these wars is now being waged. Never before, except for the ephemeral conquests of certain Asiatic barbarians, have there been subjugations of civilized peoples on so great a scale.

During this period here and there something has been done for peace, much has been done for liberty, and very much has been done for reform and advancement. But the professional pacificists, taken as a class throughout the entire period, have done nothing for permanent peace and less than nothing for liberty and for the forward movement of mankind. Hideous things have been done in the name of liberty, in the name of order, in the name of religion; and the victories that have been gained against these iniquities have been gained by strong men, armed, who put their strength at the service of righteousness and who were hampered and not helped by the futility of the men who inveighed against all use of armed strength.

The effective workers for the peace of righteousness were men like Stein, Cavour, and Lincoln; that is, men who dreamed great dreams, but who were also pre-eminently men of action, who stood for the right, and who knew that the right would fail unless might was put behind it. The prophets of pacificism have had nothing whatever in common with these great men; and whenever they have preached mere pacificism, whenever they have failed to put righteousness first and to advocate peace as the handmaiden of righteousness, they have done evil and not good.

After the exhaustion of the Napoleonic struggles there came thirty-five years during which there was no great war, while what was called "the long peace" was broken only by minor international wars or short-lived revolutionary contests. Good, but not far-sighted, men in various countries, but especially in England, Germany, and our own country, forthwith began to dream dreams – not of a universal peace that should be founded on justice and righteousness backed by strength, but of a universal peace to be obtained by the prattle of weaklings and the outpourings of amiable enthusiasts who lacked the fighting edge. About 1850, for instance, the first large peace congress was held. There were numbers of kindly people who felt that this congress, and the contemporary international exposition, also the first of its kind, heralded the beginning of a régime of universal peace. As a matter of fact, there followed twenty years during which a number of great and bloody wars took place – wars far surpassing in extent, in duration, in loss of life and property, and in importance anything that had been seen since the close of the Napoleonic contest.

Then there came another period of nearly thirty years during which there were relatively only a few wars, and these not of the highest importance. Again upright and intelligent but uninformed men began to be misled by foolish men into the belief that world peace was about to be secured, on a basis of amiable fatuity all around and under the lead of the preachers of the diluted mush of make-believe morality. A number of peace congresses, none of which accomplished anything, were held, and also certain Hague conferences, which did accomplish a certain small amount of real good but of a strictly limited kind. It was well worth going into these Hague conferences, but only on condition of clearly understanding how strictly limited was the good that they accomplished. The hysterical people who treated them as furnishing a patent peace panacea did nothing but harm, and partially offset the real but limited good the conferences actually accomplished. Indeed, the conferences undoubtedly did a certain amount of damage because of the preposterous expectations they excited among well-meaning but ill-informed and unthinking persons. These persons really believed that it was possible to achieve the millennium by means that would not have been very effective in preserving peace among the active boys of a large Sunday-school – let alone grown-up men in the world as it actually is. A pathetic commentary on their attitude is furnished by the fact that the fifteen years that have elapsed since the first Hague conference have seen an immense increase of war, culminating in the present war, waged by armies, and with bloodshed, on a scale far vaster than ever before in the history of mankind.

All these facts furnish no excuse whatever for our failing to work zealously for peace, but they absolutely require us to understand that it is noxious to work for a peace not based on righteousness, and useless to work for a peace based on righteousness unless we put force back of righteousness. At present this means that adequate preparedness against war offers to our nation its sole guarantee against wrong and aggression.

Emerson has said that in the long run the most uncomfortable truth is a safer travelling companion than the most agreeable falsehood. The advocates of peace will accomplish nothing except mischief until they are willing to look facts squarely in the face. One of these facts is that universal military service, wherever tried, has on the whole been a benefit and not a harm to the people of the nation, so long as the demand upon the average man's life has not been for too long a time. The Swiss people have beyond all question benefited by their system of limited but universal preparation for military service. The same thing is true of Australia, Chile, and Argentina. In every one of these countries the short military training given has been found to increase in marked fashion the social and industrial efficiency, the ability to do good industrial work, of the man thus trained. It would be well for the United States from every standpoint immediately to provide such strictly limited universal military training.

But it is well also for the United States to understand that a system of military training which from our standpoint would be excessive and unnecessary in order to meet our needs, may yet work admirably for some other nation. The two nations that during the last fifty years have made by far the greatest progress are Germany and Japan; and they are the two nations in which preparedness for war in time of peace has been carried to the highest point of scientific development. The feat of Japan has been something absolutely without precedent in recorded history. Great civilizations, military, industrial, and artistic, have arisen and flourished in Asia again and again in the past. But never before has an Asiatic power succeeded in adopting civilization of the European or most advanced type and in developing it to a point of military and industrial efficiency equalled only by one power of European blood.

As for Germany, we believers in democracy who also understand, as every sound-thinking democrat must, that democracy cannot succeed unless it shows the same efficiency that is shown by autocracy (as Switzerland on a small scale has shown it) need above all other men carefully to study what Germany has accomplished during the last half century. Her military efficiency has not been more astounding than her industrial and social efficiency; and the essential thing in her career of greatness has been the fact that this industrial and social efficiency is in part indirectly based upon the military efficiency and in part indirectly based upon it, because based upon the mental, physical, and moral qualities developed by the military efficiency. The solidarity and power of collective action, the trained ability to work hard for an end which is afar off in the future, the combination of intelligent forethought with efficient and strenuous action – all these together have given her her extraordinary industrial pre-eminence; and all of these have been based upon her military efficiency.

The Germans have developed patriotism of the most intense kind, and although this patriotism expresses itself in thunderous songs, in speeches and in books, it does not confine itself to these methods of expression, but treats them merely as incitements to direct and efficient action. After five months of war, Germany has on the whole been successful against opponents which in population outnumber her over two to one, and in natural resources are largely superior. Russian and French armies have from time to time obtained lodgement on German soil; but on the whole the fighting has been waged by German armies on Russian, French, and Belgian territory. On her western frontier, it is true, she was checked and thrown back after her first drive on Paris, and again checked and thrown slightly back when, after the fall of Antwerp, she attempted to advance along the Belgian coast. But in the west she has on the whole successfully pursued the offensive, and her battle lines are in the enemies' territory, although she has had to face the entire strength of France, England, and Belgium.

Moreover, she did this with only a part of her forces. At the same time she was also obliged to use immense armies, singly or in conjunction with the Austrians, against the Russians on her Eastern frontier. No one can foretell the issue of the war. But what Germany has already done must extort the heartiest admiration for her grim efficiency. It could have been done only by a masterful people guided by keen intelligence and inspired by an intensely patriotic spirit.

France has likewise shown to fine advantage in this war (in spite of certain marked shortcomings, such as the absurd uniforms of her soldiers) because of her system of universal military training. England has suffered lamentably because there has been no such system. Great masses of Englishmen, including all her men at the front, have behaved so as to command our heartiest admiration. But qualification must be made when the nation as a whole is considered. Her professional soldiers, her navy, and her upper classes have done admirably; but the English papers describe certain sections of her people as making a poor showing in their refusal to volunteer. The description of the professional football matches, attended by tens of thousands of spectators, none of whom will enlist, makes a decent man ardently wish that under a rigid conscription law the entire body of players, promoters, and spectators could be sent to the front. Scotland and Canada have apparently made an extraordinary showing; the same thing is true of sections, high and low, of society in England proper; but it is also true that certain sections of the British democracy under a system of free volunteering have shown to disadvantage compared to Germany, where military service is universal. The lack of foresight in preparation was also shown by the inability of the authorities to furnish arms and equipment for the troops that were being raised. These shortcomings are not alluded to by me in a censorious spirit, and least of all with any idea of reflecting on England, but purely that our own people may profit by the lessons taught. America should pay heed to these facts and profit by them; and we can only so profit if we realize that under like conditions we should at the moment make a much poorer showing than England has made.

It is indispensable to remember that in the cases of both Germany and Japan their extraordinary success has been due directly to that kind of efficiency in war which springs only from the highest efficiency in preparedness for war. Until educated people who sincerely desire peace face this fact with all of its implications, unpleasant and pleasant, they will not be able to better present international conditions. In order to secure this betterment, conditions must be created which will enable civilized nations to achieve such efficiency without being thereby rendered dangerous to their neighbors and to civilization as a whole. Americans, particularly, and, to a degree only slightly less, Englishmen and Frenchmen need to remember this fact, for while the ultrapacificists, the peace-at-any-price men, have appeared sporadically everywhere, they have of recent years been most numerous and noxious in the United States, in Great Britain, and in France.

Inasmuch as in our country, where, Heaven knows, we have evils enough with which to grapple, none of these evils is in even the smallest degree due to militarism – inasmuch as to inveigh against militarism in the United States is about as useful as to inveigh against eating horse-flesh in honor of Odin – this seems curious. But it is true. Probably it is merely another illustration of the old, old truth that persons who shrink from grappling with grave and real evils often strive to atone to their consciences for such failure by empty denunciation of evils which to them offer no danger and no temptation; which, as far as they are concerned, do not exist. Such denunciation is easy. It is also worthless.

American college presidents, clergymen, professors, and publicists with much pretension – some, of it founded on fact – to intelligence have praised works like that of Mr. Bloch, who "proved" that war was impossible, and like those of Mr. Norman Angell, who "proved" that it was an illusion to believe that it was profitable. The greatest and most terrible wars in history have taken place since Mr. Bloch wrote. When Mr. Angell wrote no unprejudiced man of wisdom could have failed to understand that the two most successful nations of recent times, Germany and Japan, owed their great national success to successful war. The United States owes not only its greatness but its very existence to the fact that in the Civil War the men who controlled its destinies were the fighting men. The counsels of the ultrapacificists, the peace-at-any-price men of that day, if adopted, would have meant not only the death of the nation but an incalculable disaster to humanity. A righteous war may at any moment be essential to national welfare; and it is a lamentable fact that nations have sometimes profited greatly by war that was not righteous. Such evil profit will never be done away with until armed force is put behind righteousness.

We must also remember, however, that the mischievous folly of the men whose counsels tend to inefficiency and impotence is not worse than the baseness of the men who in a spirit of mean and cringing admiration of brute force gloss over, or justify, or even deify, the exhibition of unscrupulous strength. Writings like those of Homer Lea, or of Nietzsche, or even of Professor Treitschke – not to speak of Carlyle – are as objectionable as those of Messrs. Bloch and Angell. Our people need to pay homage to the great efficiency and the intense patriotism of Germany. But they need no less fully to realize that this patriotism has at times been accompanied by callous indifference to the rights of weaker nations, and that this efficiency has at times been exercised in a way that represents a genuine setback to humanity and civilization. Germany's conduct toward Belgium can be justified only in accordance with a theory which will also justify Napoleon's conduct toward Spain and his treatment of Prussia and of all Germany during the six years succeeding Jena. I do not see how any man can fail to sympathize with Stein and Schornhorst; with Andreas Hofer, with the Maid of Saragossa, with Koerner and the Tugendbund; and if he does so sympathize, he must extend the same sympathy and admiration to King Albert and the Belgians.

Moreover, it is well for Americans always to remember that what has been done to Belgium would, of course, be done to us just as unhesitatingly if the conditions required it.

Of course, the lowest depth is reached by the professional pacificists who continue to scream for peace without daring to protest against any concrete wrong committed against peace. These include all of our fellow countrymen who at the present time clamor for peace without explicitly and clearly declaring that the first condition of peace should be the righting of the wrongs of Belgium, reparation to her, and guarantee against the possible repetition of such wrongs at the expense of any well-behaved small civilized power in the future. It may be that peace will come without such reparation and guarantee but if so it will be as emphatically the peace of unrighteousness as was the peace made at Tilsit a hundred and seven years ago.

When the President appoints a day of prayer for peace, without emphatically making it evident that the prayer should be for the redress of the wrongs without which peace would be harmful, he cannot be considered as serving righteousness. When Mr. Bryan concludes absurd all-inclusive arbitration treaties and is loquacious to peace societies about the abolition of war, without daring to protest against the hideous wrongs done Belgium, he feebly serves unrighteousness. More comic manifestations, of course entirely useless but probably too fatuous to be really mischievous, are those which find expression in the circulation of peace postage-stamps with doves on them, or in taking part in peace parades – they might as well be antivaccination parades – or in the circulation of peace petitions to be signed by schoolchildren, which for all their possible effect might just as well relate to the planet Mars.

International peace will only come when the nations of the world form some kind of league which provides for an international tribunal to decide on international matters, which decrees that treaties and international agreements are never to be entered into recklessly and foolishly, and when once entered into are to be observed with entire good faith, and which puts the collective force of civilization behind such treaties and agreements and court decisions and against any wrong-doing or recalcitrant nation. The all-inclusive arbitration treaties negotiated by the present administration amount to almost nothing. They are utterly worthless for good. They are however slightly mischievous because:

1. There is no provision for their enforcement, and,

2. They would be in some cases not only impossible but improper to enforce.

A treaty is a promise. It is like a promise to pay in the commercial world. Its value lies in the means provided for redeeming the promise. To make it, and not redeem it, is vicious. A United States gold certificate is valuable because gold is back of it. If there were nothing back of it the certificate would sink to the position of fiat money, which is irredeemable, and therefore valueless; as in the case of our Revolutionary currency. The Wilson-Bryan all-inclusive arbitration treaties represent nothing whatever but international fiat money. To make them is no more honest than it is to issue fiat money. Mr. Bryan would not make a good Secretary of the Treasury, but he would do better in that position than as Secretary of State. For his type of fiat obligations is a little worse in international than in internal affairs. The all-inclusive arbitration treaties, in whose free and unlimited negotiation Mr. Bryan takes such pleasure, are of less value than the thirty-cent dollars, whose free and unlimited coinage he formerly advocated.

An efficient world league for peace is as yet in the future; and it may be, although I sincerely hope not, in the far future. The indispensable thing for every free people to do in the present day is with efficiency to prepare against war by making itself able physically to defend its rights and by cultivating that stern and manly spirit without which no material preparation will avail.

The last point is all essential. It is not of much use to provide an armed force if that force is composed of poltroons and ultrapacificists.

Such men should be sent to the front, of course, for they should not be allowed to shirk the danger which their braver fellow countrymen willingly face, and under proper discipline some use can be made of them; but the fewer there are of them in a nation the better the army of that nation will be.

A Yale professor – he might just as well have been a Harvard professor – is credited in the press with saying the other day that he wishes the United States would take the position that if attacked it would not defend itself, and would submit unresistingly to any spoliation. The professor said that this would afford such a beautiful example to mankind that war would undoubtedly be abolished. Magazine writers, and writers of syndicate articles published in reputable papers, have recently advocated similar plans. Men who talk this way are thoroughly bad citizens. Few members of the criminal class are greater enemies of the republic.

American citizens must understand that they cannot advocate or acquiesce in an evil course of action and then escape responsibility for the results. If disaster comes to our navy in the near future it will be directly due to the way the navy has been handled during the past twenty-two months, and a part of the responsibility will be shared by every man who has failed effectively to protest against, or in any way has made himself responsible for, the attitude of the present administration in foreign affairs and as regards the navy.

The first and most important thing for us as a people to do, in order to prepare ourselves for self-defense, is to get clearly in our minds just what our policy is to be, and to insist that our public servants shall make their words and their deeds correspond. As has already been pointed out, the present administration was elected on the explicit promise that the Philippines should be given their independence, and it has taken action in the Philippines which can only be justified on the theory that this independence is to come in the immediate future. I believe that we have rendered incalculable service to the Philippines, and that what we have there done has shown in the most striking manner the extreme mischief that would have followed if, in 1898 and the subsequent years, we had failed to do our duty in consequence of following the advice of Mr. Bryan and the pacificists or anti-imperialists of that day. But we must keep our promises; and we ought now to leave the islands completely at as early a date as possible.

There remains to defend – the United States proper, the Panama Canal and its approaches, Alaska, and Hawaii. To defend all these is vital to our honor and interest. For such defense preparedness is essential.

The first and most essential form of preparedness should be making the navy efficient. Absolutely and relatively, our navy has never been at such a pitch of efficiency as in February, 1909, when the battle fleet returned from its voyage around the world. Unit for unit, there was no other navy in the world which was at that time its equal. During the next four years we had an admirable Secretary of the Navy, Mr. Meyer – we were fortunate in having then and since good Secretaries of War in Mr. Stimson and Mr. Garrison. Owing to causes for which Mr. Meyer was in no way responsible, there was a slight relative falling off in the efficiency of the navy, and probably a slight absolute falling off during the following four years. But it remained very efficient.

Since Mr. Daniels came in, and because of the action taken by Mr. Daniels under the direction of President Wilson, there has been a most lamentable reduction in efficiency. If at this moment we went to war with a first-class navy of equal strength to our own, there would be a chance not only of defeat but of disgrace. It is probably impossible to put the navy in really first-class condition with Mr. Daniels at its head, precisely as it is impossible to conduct our foreign affairs with dignity and efficiency while Mr. Bryan is at the head of the State Department.

But the great falling-off in naval efficiency has been due primarily to the policy pursued by President Wilson himself. He has kept the navy in Mexican waters. The small craft at Tampico and elsewhere could have rendered real service, but the President refused to allow them to render such service, and left English and German sea officers to protect our people. The great war craft were of no use at all; yet at this moment he has brought back from Mexico the army which could be of some use and has kept there the war-ships which cannot be of any use, and which suffer terribly in efficiency from being so kept. The fleet has had no manœuvring for twenty-two months. It has had almost no gun practice by division during that time. There is not enough powder; there are not enough torpedoes; the bottoms of the ships are foul; there are grave defects in the submarines; there is a deficiency in aircraft; the under-enlistments indicate a deficiency of from ten thousand to twenty thousand men; the whole service is being handled in such manner as to impair its fitness and morale.

Congress should summon before its committees the best naval experts and provide the battleships, cruisers, submarines, floating mines, and aircraft that these experts declare to be necessary for the full protection of the United States. It should bear in mind that while many of these machines of war are essentially to be used in striking from the coasts themselves, yet that others must be designed to keep the enemy afar from these coasts. Mere defensive by itself cannot permanently avail. The only permanently efficient defensive arm is one which can act offensively. Our navy must be fitted for attack, for delivering smashing blows, in order effectively to defend our own shores. Above all, we should remember that a highly trained personnel is absolutely indispensable, for without it no material preparation is of the least avail.

But the navy alone will not suffice in time of great crisis. If England had adopted the policy urged by Lord Roberts, there would probably have been no war and certainly the war would now have been at an end, as she would have been able to protect Belgium, as well as herself, and to save France from invasion. Relatively to the Continent, England was utterly unprepared; but she was a miracle of preparedness compared to us. There are many ugly features connected with the slowness of certain sections of the English people to volunteer and with their deficiency in rifles, horses, and equipment; and there have been certain military and naval shortcomings; but until we have radically altered our habits of thought and action we can only say with abashed humility that if England has not shown to advantage compared to Germany, she has certainly done far better than we would have done, and than, as a matter of fact, we actually have done during the past twenty-two months, both as regards Mexico and as regards the fulfilment of our duty in the situation created by the world war.

Congress should at once act favorably along the lines recommended in the recent excellent report of the Secretary of War and in accordance with the admirable plan outlined in the last report of the Chief of Staff of the army, General Wotherspoon – a report with which his predecessor as Chief of Staff, General Wood, appears to be in complete sympathy. Our army should be doubled in size. An effective reserve should be created. Every year there should be field manœuvres on a large scale, a hundred thousand being engaged for several weeks. The artillery should be given the most scientific training. The equipment should be made perfect at every point. Rigid economy should be demanded.

Every officer and man should be kept to the highest standard of physical and moral fitness. The unfit should be ruthlessly weeded out. At least one third of the officers in each grade should be promoted on merit without regard to seniority, and the least fit for promotion should be retired. Every unit of the regular army and reserve should be trained to the highest efficiency under war conditions.

But this is not enough. There should be at least ten times the number of riflses and the quantity of ammunition in the country that there are now. In our high schools and colleges a system of military training like that which obtains in Switzerland and Australia should be given. Furthermore, all our young men should be trained in actual field-service under war conditions; preferably on the Swiss, but if not on the Swiss then on the Argentinian or Chilean model.

The Swiss model would probably be better for our people. It would necessitate only four to six months' service shortly after graduation from high school or college, and thereafter only about eight days a year. No man could buy a substitute; no man would be excepted because of his wealth; all would serve in the ranks on precisely the same terms side by side.

Under this system the young men would be trained to shoot, to march, to take care of themselves in the open, and to learn those habits of self-reliance and law-abiding obedience which are not only essential to the efficiency of a citizen soldiery, but are no less essential to the efficient performance of civic duties in a free democracy. My own firm belief is that this system would help us in civil quite as much as in military matters. It would increase our social and industrial efficiency. It would help us to habits of order and respect for law.

This proposal does not represent anything more than carrying out the purpose of the second amendment to the Federal Constitution, which declares that a well-regulated militia is necessary to the security of a free nation. The Swiss army is a well-regulated militia; and, therefore it is utterly different from any militia we have ever had. The system of compulsory training and universal service has worked admirably in Switzerland. It has saved the Swiss from war. It has developed their efficiency in peace.

In theory, President Wilson advocates unpreparedness, and in the actual fact he practises, on our behalf, tame submission to wrong-doing and refusal to stand for our own rights or for the rights of any weak power that is wronged. We who take the opposite view advocate merely acting as Washington urged us to act, when in his first annual address he said: "To be prepared for war is one of the most effectual means for preserving peace. A free people ought not only to be armed but disciplined; to which end a uniform and well-digested plan is requisite." Jefferson was not a fighting man, but even Jefferson, writing to Monroe in 1785, urged the absolute need of building up our navy if we wished to escape oppression to our commerce and "the present disrespect of the nations of Europe," and added the pregnant sentence: "A coward is much more exposed to quarrels than a man of spirit." As President, he urged our people to train themselves to arms, so as to constitute a citizen soldiery, in terms that showed that his object was to accomplish exactly what the Swiss have accomplished, and what is advocated in this book. In one annual message he advocated "the organization of 300,000 able-bodied men between the ages of eighteen and twenty-five for offense or defense at any time or in any place where they may be wanted." In a letter to Monroe he advocated compulsory military service, saying: "We must train and classify the whole of our male citizenry and make military instruction a part of collegiate education. We can never be safe until this is done." The methods taken by Jefferson and the Americans of Jefferson's day to accomplish this object were fatally defective. But their purpose was the same that those who think as we do now put forward. The difference is purely that we present efficient methods for accomplishing this purpose. Washington was a practical man of high ideals who always strove to reduce his ideals to practice. His address to Congress in December, 1793, ought to have been read by President Wilson before the latter sent in his message of 1914 with its confused advocacy of unpreparedness and its tone of furtive apology for submission to insult. Washington said: "There is much due to the United States among nations which will be withheld, if not absolutely lost, by the reputation of weakness. If we desire to avoid insult, we must be able to repel it. If we desire to secure peace ... it must be known that we are at all times ready for war," and he emphasized the fact that the peace thus secured by preparedness for war is the most potent method of obtaining material prosperity.

The need of such a system as that which I advocate is well brought out in a letter I recently received from a college president. It runs in part as follows:

What the average young fellow of eighteen to thirty doesn't know about shooting and riding makes an appalling total. I remember very well visiting the First Connecticut Regiment a day or two before it left for service in the Spanish War. A good many of my boys were with them and I went to see them off. One fellow in particular, of whom I was and am very fond, took me to his tent and proudly exhibited his rifle, calling attention to the beautiful condition to which he had brought it. It certainly was extremely shiny, and I commended him for his careful cleansing of his death-dealing weapon. Then I discovered that the firing-pin (it was an old Springfield) was rusted immovably into its place, and that my boy didn't know that there was any firing-pin. He had learned to expect that if you put a cartridge into the breech, pulled down the block, and pulled the trigger, it would probably go off if he had previously cocked it; but he had never done any of these things.

It was my fortune to grow up amid surroundings and in a time when every boy had and used a gun. Any boy fourteen years old who was not the proprietor of some kind of shooting-iron and fairly proficient in its use was in disgrace. Such a situation was unthinkable. So we were all fairly dependable shots with a fowling-piece or rifle. As a result of this and subsequent experience, I really believe that so long as my aging body would endure hardship, and provided further that I could be prevented from running away, I should be a more efficient soldier than most of the young fellows on our campus to-day.

I have watched with much dissatisfaction the gradual disappearance of the military schools here in the East. There are some prominent and useful ones in the West, but they are far too few, and I do not believe there is any preliminary military training of any sort in our public schools. I fear that the military training required by law in certain agricultural and other schools receiving federal aid is more or less of a fake; the object seeming to be to get the appropriation and make the least possible return.

If in any way you can bring it about that our boys shall be taught to shoot, I believe with you that they can learn the essentials of drill very quickly when need arises. And even so, however, our rulers must learn the necessity of having rifles enough and ammunition enough to meet any emergency at all likely to occur.

It is idle for this nation to trust to arbitration and neutrality treaties unbacked by force. It is idle to trust to the tepid good-will of other nations. It is idle to trust to alliances. Alliances change. Russia and Japan are now fighting side by side, although nine years ago they were fighting against one another. Twenty years ago Russia and Germany stood side by side. Fifteen years ago England was more hostile to Russia, and even to France, than she was to Germany. It is perfectly possible that after the close of this war the present allies will fall out, or that Germany and Japan will turn up in close alliance.

It is our duty to try to work for a great world league for righteous peace enforced by power; but no such league is yet in sight. At present the prime duty of the American people is to abandon the inane and mischievous principle of watchful waiting – that is, of slothful and timid refusal either to face facts or to perform duty. Let us act justly toward others; and let us also be prepared with stout heart and strong hand to defend our rights against injustice from others.

In his recent report the Secretary of War, Mr. Garrison, has put the case for preparedness in the interest of honorable peace so admirably that what he says should be studied by all our people. It runs in part as follows:

"This, then, leaves for consideration the imminent questions of military policy; the considerations which, in my view, should be taken into account in determining the same; and the suggestions which occur to me to be pertinent in the circumstances.

It would be premature to attempt now to draw the ultimate lessons from the war in Europe. It is an imperative duty, however, to heed so much of what it brings home to us as is incontrovertible and not to be changed by any event, leaving for later and more detailed and comprehensive consideration what its later developments and final conclusions may indicate.

For orderly treatment certain preliminary considerations may be usefully adverted to. It is, of course, not necessary to dwell on the blessings of peace and the horrors of war. Every one desires peace, just as every one desires health, contentment, affection, sufficient means for comfortable existence, and other similarly beneficent things. But peace and the other states of being just mentioned are not always or even often solely within one's own control. Those who are thoughtful and have courage face the facts of life, take lessons from experience, and strive by wise conduct to attain the desirable things, and by provision and precaution to protect and defend them when obtained. It may truthfully be said that eternal vigilance is the price which must be paid in order to obtain the desirable things of life and to defend them.

In collective affairs the interests of the group are confided to the government, and it thereupon is charged with the duty to preserve and defend these things. The government must exercise for the nation the precautionary, defensive, and preservative measures necessary to that end. All governments must therefore have force – physical force – *i.e.*, military force, for these purposes. The question for each nation when this matter is under consideration is, How much force should it have and of what should that force consist?

In the early history of our nation there was a natural, almost inevitable, abhorrence of military force, because it connoted military despotism. Most, if not all, of the early settlers in this country came from nations where a few powerful persons tyrannically imposed their will upon the people by means of military power. The consequence was that the oppressed who fled to this country neces-sarily connected military force with despotism and had a dread the-reof. Of course, all this has long since passed into history. No reaso-nable person in this country to-day has the slightest shadow of fear of military despotism, nor of any interference whatever by military force in the conduct of civil affairs. The military and the civil are just as completely and permanently separated in this country as the church and the state are; the subjection of the military to the civil is settled and unchangeable. The only reason for adverting to the obsolete condition is to anticipate the action of those who will cite from the works of the founders of the republic excerpts showing a dread of military ascendancy in our government. Undoubtedly, at the time such sentiments were expressed there was a very real dread. At the present time such expressions are entirely inapplicable and do not furnish even a presentable pretext for opposing proper military preparation.

It also seems proper, in passing, to refer to the frame of mind of those who use the word "militarism" as the embodiment of the doc-trine of brute force and loosely apply it to any organized prepara-tion of military force, and therefore deprecate any adequate military preparation because it is a step in the direction of the contemned "militarism." It is perfectly apparent to any one who approaches the matter with an unprejudiced mind that what constitutes undesira-ble militarism, as distinguished from a necessary, proper, and ade-quate preparation of the military resources of the nation, depends upon the position in which each nation finds itself, and varies with every nation and with different conditions in each nation at diffe-rent times. Every nation must have adequate force to protect itself from domestic insurrections, to enforce its laws, and to repel invasi-ons; that is, every nation that has similar characteristics to those of a self-respecting man. (The Constitution obliges the United States to protect each State against invasion.) If it prepares and maintains more military force than is necessary for the purposes just named, then it is subject to the conviction, in the public opinion of the world, of having embraced "militarism," unless it intends aggression for a cause which the public opinion of the world conceives to be a righteous one. To the extent, however, that it confines its military preparedness to the purposes first mentioned, there is neither warrant nor justification in characterizing such action as "militarism." Those who would thus characterize it do so because they have reached the conclusion that a nation to-day can properly dispense with a prepared military force, and therefore they apply the word to any preparation or organization of the military resources of the nation. Not being able to conceive how a reasonable, prudent, patriotic man can reach such a conclusion, I cannot conceive any arguments or statements that would alter such a state of mind. It disregards all known facts, flies in the face of all experience, and must rest upon faith in that which has not yet been made manifest.

Whatever the future may hold in the way of agreements between nations, followed by actual disarmament thereof, of international courts of arbitration, and other greatly-to-be-desired measures to lessen or prevent conflict between nation and nation, we all know that at present these conditions are not existing. We can and will eagerly adept ourselves to each beneficent development along these lines; but to merely enfeeble ourselves in the meantime would, in my view, be unthinkable folly. By neglecting and refusing to provide ourselves with the necessary means of self-protection and self-defense we could not hasten or in any way favorably influence the ultimate results we desire in these respects."

Chapter XI

Utopia or Hell?

Sherman's celebrated declaration about war has certainly been borne out by what has happened in Europe, and above all in Belgium, during the last four months. That war is hell I will concede as heartily as any ultrapacificist. But the only alternative to war, that is to hell, is the adoption of some plan substantially like that which I herein advocate and which has itself been called utopian. It is possible that it is utopian for the time being; that is, that nations are not ready as yet to accept it. But it is also possible that after this war has come to an end the European contestants will be sufficiently sobered to be willing to consider some such proposal, and that the United States will abandon the folly of the pacificists and be willing to cooperate in some practical effort for the only kind of peace worth having, the peace of justice and righteousness.

The proposal is not in the least utopian, if by utopian we understand something that is theoretically desirable but impossible. What I propose is a working and realizable Utopia. My proposal is that the efficient civilized nations – those that are efficient in war as well as in peace – shall join in a world league for the peace of righteousness. This means that they shall by solemn covenant agree as to their respective rights which shall not be questioned; that they shall agree that all other questions arising between them shall be submitted to a court of arbitration; and that they shall also agree – and here comes the vital and essential point of the whole system – to act with the combined military strength of all of them against any recalcitrant nation, against any nation which transgresses at the expense of any other nation the rights which it is agreed shall not be questioned, or which on arbitrable matters refuses to submit to the decree of the arbitral court.

In its essence this plan means that there shall be a great international treaty for the peace of righteousness; that this treaty shall explicitly secure to each nation and except from the operations of any international tribunal such matters as its territorial integrity, honor, and vital interest, and shall guarantee it in the possession of these rights; that this treaty shall therefore by its own terms explicitly provide against making foolish promises which cannot and ought not to be kept; that this treaty shall be observed with absolute good faith – for it is worse than useless to enter into treaties until their observance in good faith is efficiently secured. Finally, and most important, this treaty shall put force back of righteousness, shall provide a method of securing by the exercise of force the observance of solemn international obligations. This is to be accomplished by all the powers covenanting to put their whole strength back of the fulfilment of the treaty obligations, including the decrees of the court established under and in accordance with the treaty.

This proposal, therefore, meets the well-found objections against the foolish and mischievous all-inclusive arbitration treaties recently negotiated by Mr. Bryan under the direction of President Wilson. These treaties, like the all-inclusive arbitration treaties which President Taft started to negotiate, explicitly include as arbitrable, or as proper subjects for action by joint commissions, questions of honor and of vital national interest. No such provision should be made. No such provision is made as among private individuals in any civilized community. No man is required to "arbitrate" a slap in the face or an insult to his wife; no man is expected to "arbitrate" with a burglar or a highwayman. If in private life one individual takes action which immediately jeopardizes the life or limb or even the bodily well-being and the comfort of another, the wronged party does not have to go into any arbitration with the wrong-doer. On the contrary, the policeman or constable or sheriff immediately and summarily arrests the wrong-doer. The subsequent trial is not in the nature of arbitration at all. It is in the nature of a criminal proceeding. The wronged man is merely a witness and not necessarily an essential witness. For example, if, in the streets of New York, one man assaults another or steals his watch, and a policeman is not near by, the wronged man is not only justified in knocking down the assailant or thief, but fails in his duty if he does not so act. If a policeman is near by, the policeman promptly arrests the wrong-doer. The magistrate does not arbitrate the question of property rights in the watch nor anything about the assault. He satisfies himself as to the facts and delivers judgment against the offender.

A covenant between the United States and any other power to arbitrate all questions, including those involving national honor and interest, neither could nor ought to be kept. Such a covenant will be harmless only if no such questions ever arise. Now, all the worth of promises made in the abstract lies in the way in which they are fulfilled in the concrete. The Wilson-Bryan arbitration treaties are to be tested in this manner. The theory is, of course, that these treaties are to be made with all nations, and this is correct, because it would be a far graver thing to refuse to make them with some nations than to refuse to enter into them with any nation at all. The proposal is, in effect, and disregarding verbiage, that all questions shall be arbitrated or settled by the action of a joint commission – questions really vital to us would, as a matter of fact, be settled adversely to us pending such action. There are many such questions which in the concrete we would certainly not arbitrate. I mention one, only as an example. Do Messrs. Wilson and Bryan, or do they not, mean to arbitrate, if Japan should so desire, the question whether Japanese laborers are to be allowed to come in unlimited numbers to these shores? If they do mean this, let them explicitly state that fact – merely as an illustration – to the Senate committee, so that the Senate committee shall understand what it is doing when it ratifies these treaties. If they do not mean this, then let them promptly withdraw all the treaties so as not to expose us to the charge of hypocrisy, of making believe to do what we have no intention of doing, and of making promises which we have no intention of keeping. I have mentioned one issue only; but there are scores of other issues which I could mention which this government would under no circumstances agree to arbitrate.

In the same way, we must explicitly recognize that all the peace congresses and the like that have been held of recent years have done no good whatever to the cause of world peace. All their addresses and resolutions about arbitration and disarmament and such matters have been on the whole slightly worse than useless. Disregarding the Hague conventions, it is the literal fact that none of the peace congresses that have been held for the last fifteen or twenty years – to speak only of those of which I myself know the workings – have accomplished the smallest particle of good. In so far as they have influenced free, liberty-loving, and self-respecting nations not to take measures for their own defense they have been positively mischievous. In no respect have they achieved anything worth achieving; and the present world war proves this beyond the possibility of serious question.

The Hague conventions stand by themselves. They have accomplished a certain amount – although only a small amount – of actual good. This was in so far as they furnished means by which nations which did not wish to quarrel were able to settle international disputes not involving their deepest interests. Questions between nations continually arise which are not of first-class importance; which, for instance, refer to some illegal act by or against a fishing schooner, to some difficulty concerning contracts, to some question of the interpretation of a minor clause in a treaty, or to the sporadic action of some hot-headed or panic-struck official. In these cases, where neither nation wishes to go to war, the Hague court has furnished an easy method for the settlement of the dispute without war. This does not mark a very great advance; but it is an advance, and was worth making.

The fact that it is the only advance that the Hague court has accomplished makes the hysterical outbursts formerly indulged in by the ultrapacificists concerning it seem in retrospect exceedingly foolish. While I had never shared the hopes of these ultrapacificists, I had hoped for more substantial good than has actually come from the Hague conventions. This was because I accept promises as meaning something. The ultrapacificists, whether from timidity, from weakness, or from sheer folly, seem wholly unable to understand that the fulfilment of a promise has anything to do with making the promise. The most striking example that could possibly be furnished has been furnished by Belgium. Under my direction as President, the United States signed the Hague conventions. All the nations engaged in the present war signed these conventions, although one or two of the nations qualified their acceptance, or withheld their signatures to certain articles. This, however, did not in the least relieve the signatory powers from the duty to guarantee one another in the enjoyment of the rights supposed to be secured by the conventions. To make this guarantee worth anything, it was, of course, necessary actively to enforce it against any power breaking the convention or acting against its clear purpose. To make it really effective it should be enforced as quickly against non-signatory as against signatory powers; for to give a power free permission to do wrong if it did not sign would put a premium on non-signing, so far as big, aggressive powers are concerned.

I authorized the signature of the United States to these conventions. They forbid the violation of neutral territory, and, of course, the subjugation of unoffending neutral nations, as Belgium has been subjugated. They forbid such destruction as that inflicted on Louvain, Dinant, and other towns in Belgium, the burning of their priceless public libraries and wonderful halls and churches, and the destruction of cathedrals such as that at Rheims. They forbid the infliction of heavy pecuniary penalties and the taking of severe punitive measures at the expense of civilian populations. They forbid the bombardment – of course including the dropping of bombs from aeroplanes – of unfortified cities and of cities whose defenses were not at the moment attacked. They forbid such actions as have been committed against various cities, Belgian, French, and English, not for military reason but for the purpose of terrorizing the civilian population by killing and wounding men, women, and children who were non-combatants. All of these offenses have been committed by Germany. I took the action I did in directing these conventions to be signed on the theory and with the belief that the United States intended to live up to its obligations, and that our people understood that living up to solemn obligations, like any other serious performance of duty, means willingness to make effort and to incur risk. If I had for one moment supposed that signing these Hague conventions meant literally nothing whatever beyond the expression of a pious wish which any power was at liberty to disregard with impunity, in accordance with the dictation of self-interest, I would certainly not have permitted the United States to be a party to such a mischievous farce. President Wilson and Secretary Bryan, however, take the view that when the United States assumes obligations in order to secure small and unoffending neutral nations or non-combatants generally against hideous wrong, its action is not predicated on any intention to make the guarantee effective. They take the view that when we are asked to redeem in the concrete, promises we made in the abstract, our duty is to disregard our obligations and to preserve ignoble peace for ourselves by regarding with cold-blooded and timid indifference the most frightful ravages of war committed at the expense of a peaceful and unoffending country. This is the cult of cowardice. That Messrs. Wilson and Bryan profess it and put it in action would be of small consequence if only they themselves were concerned. The importance of their action is that it commits the United States.

Elaborate technical arguments have been made to justify this timid and selfish abandonment of duty, this timid and selfish failure to work for the world peace of righteousness, by President Wilson and Secretary Bryan. No sincere believer in disinterested and self-sacrificing work for peace can justify it; and work for peace will never be worth much unless accompanied by courage, effort, and self-sacrifice. Yet those very apostles of pacificism who, when they can do so with safety, scream loudest for peace, have made themselves objects of contemptuous derision by keeping silence in this crisis, or even by praising Mr. Wilson and Mr. Bryan for having thus abandoned the cause of peace. They are supported by the men who insist that all that we are concerned with is escaping even the smallest risk that might follow upon the performance of duty to any one except ourselves. This last is not a very exalted plea. It is, however, defensible. But if, as a nation, we intend to act in accordance with it, we must never promise to do anything for any one else.

The technical arguments as to the Hague conventions not requiring us to act will at once be brushed aside by any man who honestly and in good faith faces the situation. Either the Hague conventions meant something or else they meant nothing. If, in the event of their violation, none of the signatory powers were even to protest, then of course they meant nothing; and it was an act of unspeakable silliness to enter into them. If, on the other hand, they meant anything whatsoever, it was the duty of the United States, as the most powerful, or at least the richest and most populous, neutral nation, to take action for upholding them when their violation brought such appalling disaster to Belgium. There is no escape from this alternative.

The first essential to working out successfully any scheme whatever for world peace is to understand that nothing can be accomplished unless the powers entering into the agreement act in precisely the reverse way from that in which President Wilson and Secretary Bryan have acted as regards the Hague conventions and the all-inclusive arbitration treaties during the past six months. The prime fact to consider in securing any peace agreement worth entering into, or that will have any except a mischievous effect, is that the nations entering into the agreement shall make no promises that ought not to be made, that they shall in good faith live up to the promises that are made, and that they shall put their whole strength unitedly back of these promises against any nation which refuses to carry out the agreement, or which, if it has not made the agreement, nevertheless violates the principles which the agreement enforces. In other words, international agreements intended to produce peace must proceed much along the lines of the Hague conventions; but a power signing them, as the United States signed the Hague conventions, must do so with the intention in good faith to see that they are carried out, and to use force to accomplish this, if necessary.

To violate these conventions, to violate neutrality treaties, as Germany has done in the case of Belgium, is a dreadful wrong. It represents the gravest kind of international wrong-doing. But it is really not quite so contemptible, it does not show such short-sighted and timid inefficiency, *and, above all, such selfish indifference to the cause of permanent and righteous peace* as has been shown by us of the United States (thanks to President Wilson and Secretary Bryan) in refusing to fulfil our solemn obligations by taking whatever action was necessary in order to clear our skirts from the guilt of tame acquiescence in a wrong which we had solemnly undertaken to oppose.

It has been a matter of very real regret to me to have to speak in the way I have felt obliged to speak as to German wrong-doing in Belgium, because so many of my friends, not only Germans, but Americans of German birth and even Americans of German descent, have felt aggrieved at my position. As regards my friends, the Americans of German birth or descent, I can only say that they are in honor bound to regard all international matters solely from the standpoint of the interest of the United States, and of the demands of a lofty international morality. I recognize no divided allegiance in American citizenship. As regards Germany, my stand is for the real interest of the mass of the German people. If the German people as a whole would only look at it rightly, they would see that my position is predicated upon the assumption that we ought to act as unhesitatingly in favor of Germany if Germany were wronged as in favor of Belgium when Belgium is wronged.

There are in Germany a certain number of Germans who adopt the Treitschke and Bernhardi view of Germany's destiny and of international morality generally. These men are fundamentally exactly as hostile to America as to all other foreign powers. They look down with contempt upon Americans as well as upon all other foreigners. They regard it as their right to subdue these inferior beings. They acknowledge toward them no duty, in the sense that duty is understood between equals. I call the attention of my fellow Americans of German origin who wish this country to act toward Belgium, not in accordance with American traditions, interests, and ideals, but in accordance with the pro-German sympathies of certain citizens of German descent, to the statement of Treitschke that "to civilization at large the [Americanizing] of the German-Americans means a heavy loss. Among Germans there can no longer be any question that the civilization of mankind suffers every time a German is transformed into a Yankee."

I do not for one moment believe that the men who follow Treitschke in his hatred of and contempt for all non-Germans, and Bernhardi in his contempt for international morality, are a majority of the German people or even a very large minority. I think that the great majority of the Germans, who have approved Germany's action toward Belgium, have been influenced by the feeling that it was a vital necessity in order to save Germany from destruction and subjugation by France and Russia, perhaps assisted by England. Fear of national destruction will prompt men to do almost anything, and the proper remedy for outsiders to work for is the removal of the fear. If Germany were absolutely freed from danger of aggression on her eastern and western frontiers, I believe that German public sentiment would refuse to sanction such acts as those against Belgium. The only effective way to free it from this fear is to have outside nations like the United States in good faith undertake the obligation to defend Germany's honor and territorial integrity, if attacked, exactly as they would defend the honor and territorial integrity of Belgium, or of France, Russia, Japan, or England, or any other well-behaved, civilized power, if attacked.

This can only be achieved by some such world league of peace as that which I advocate. Most important of all, it can only be achieved by the willingness and ability of great, free powers to put might back of right, to make their protest against wrong-doing effective by, if necessary, punishing the wrong-doer. It is this fact which makes the clamor of the pacificists for "peace, peace," without any regard to righteousness, so abhorrent to all right-thinking people. There are multitudes of professional pacificists in the United States, and of well-meaning but ill-informed persons who sympathize with them from ignorance. There are not a few astute persons, bankers of foreign birth, and others, who wish to take sinister advantage of the folly of these persons, in the interest of Germany. All of these men clamor for immediate peace. They wish the United States to take action for immediate peace or for a truce, under conditions designed to leave Belgium with her wrongs unredressed and in the possession of Germany. They strive to bring about a peace which would contain within itself the elements of frightful future disaster, by making no effective provision to prevent the repetition of such wrong-doing as has been inflicted upon Belgium. All of the men advocating such action, including the professional pacificists, the big business men largely of foreign birth, and the well-meaning but feeble-minded creatures among their allies, and including especially all those who from sheer timidity or weakness shrink from duty, occupy a thoroughly base and improper position. The peace advocates of this stamp stand on an exact par with men who, if there was an epidemic of lawlessness in New York, should come together to demand the immediate cessation of all activity by the police, and should propose to substitute for it a request that the highwaymen, white slavers, black-handers, and burglars cease their activities for the moment on condition of retaining undisturbed possession of the ill-gotten spoils they had already acquired. The only effective friend of peace in a big city is the man who makes the police force thoroughly efficient, who tries to remove the causes of crime, but who unhesitatingly insists upon the punishment of criminals. Pacificists who believe that all use of force in international matters can be abolished will do well to remember that the only efficient police forces are those whose members are scrupulously careful not to commit acts of violence when it is possible to avoid them, but who are willing and able, when the occasion arises, to subdue the worst kind of wrong-doers by means of the only argument that wrong-doers respect, namely, successful force. What is thus true in private life is similarly true in international affairs.

No man can venture to state the exact details that should be followed in securing such a world league for the peace of righteousness. But, not to leave the matter nebulous, I submit the following plan. It would prove entirely workable, if nations entered into it with good faith, and if they treated their obligations under it in the spirit in which the United States treated its obligations as regarded the independence of Cuba, giving good government to the Philippines, and building the Panama Canal; the same spirit in which England acted when the neutrality of Belgium was violated.

All the civilized powers which are able and willing to furnish and to use force, when force is required to back up righteousness – and only the civilized powers who possess virile manliness of character and the willingness to accept risk and labor when necessary to the performance of duty are entitled to be considered in this matter – should join to create an international tribunal and to provide rules in accordance with which that tribunal should act. These rules would have to accept the *status quo* at some given period; for the endeavor to redress all historical wrongs would throw us back into chaos. They would lay down the rule that the territorial integrity of each nation was inviolate; that it was to be guaranteed absolutely its sovereign rights in certain particulars, including, for instance, the right to decide the terms on which immigrants should be admitted to its borders for purposes of residence, citizenship, or business; in short, all its rights in matters affecting its honor and vital interest. Each nation should be guaranteed against having any of these specified rights infringed upon. They would not be made arbitrable, any more than an individual's right to life and limb is made arbitrable; they would be mutually guaranteed. All other matters that could arise between these nations should be settled by the international court. The judges should act not as national representatives, but purely as judges; and in any given case it would probably be well to choose them by lot, excluding, of course, the representatives of the powers whose interests were concerned. Then, and most important, the nations should severally guarantee to use their entire military force, if necessary, against any nation which defied the decrees of the tribunal or which violated any of the rights which in the rules it was expressly stipulated should be reserved to the several nations, the rights to their territorial integrity and the like. Under such conditions – to make matters concrete – Belgium would be safe from any attack such as that made by Germany, and Germany would be relieved from the haunting fear its people now have lest the Russians and the French, backed by other nations, smash the empire and its people.

In addition to the contracting powers, a certain number of outside nations should be named as entitled to the benefits of the court. These nations should be chosen from those which are as civilized and well-behaved as the great contracting nations, but which, for some reason or other, are unwilling or unable to guarantee to help execute the decrees of the court by force. They would have no right to take part in the nomination of judges, for no people are entitled to do anything toward establishing a court unless they are able and willing to face the risk, labor, and self-sacrifice necessary in order to put police power behind the court. But they would be treated with exact justice; and in the event of any one of the great contracting powers having trouble with one of them, they would be entitled to go into court, have a decision rendered, and see the decision supported, precisely as in the case of a dispute between any two of the great contracting powers themselves.

No power should be admitted into the first circle, that of the contracting powers, unless it is civilized, well-behaved, and able to do its part in enforcing the decrees of the court. China, for instance, could not be admitted, nor could Turkey, although for different reasons, whereas such nations as Germany, France, England, Italy, Russia, the United States, Japan, Brazil, the Argentine, Chile, Uruguay, Switzerland, Holland, Sweden, Norway, Denmark, and Belgium would all be entitled to go in. If China continues to behave as well as it has during the last few years it might soon go into the second line of powers which would be entitled to the benefits of the court, although not entitled to send judges to it. Mexico would, of course, not be entitled to admission at present into either circle. At present every European power with the exception of Turkey would be so entitled; but sixty years ago the kingdom of Naples, for instance, would not have been entitled to come in, and there are various South American communities which at the present time would not be entitled to come in; and, of course, this would at present be true of most independent Asiatic states and of all independent African states. The council should have power to exclude any nation which completely fell from civilization, as Mexico, partly with the able assistance of President Wilson's administration, has fallen during the past few years. There are various South and Central American states which have never been entitled to the consideration as civilized, orderly, self-respecting powers which would entitle them to be treated on terms of equality in the fashion indicated. As regards these disorderly and weak outsiders, it might well be that after a while some method would be devised to deal with them by common agreement of the civilized powers; but until this was devised and put into execution they would have to be left as at present.

Of course, grave difficulties would be encountered in devising such a plan and in administering it afterward, and no human being can guarantee that it would absolutely succeed. But I believe that it could be made to work and that it would mark a very great improvement over what obtains now. At this moment there is hell in Belgium and hell in Mexico; and the ultrapacificists in this country have their full share of the responsibility for this hell. They are not primary factors in producing it. They lack the virile power to be primary factors in producing anything, good or evil, that needs daring and endurance. But they are secondary factors; for the man who tamely acquiesces in wrong-doing is a secondary factor in producing that wrong-doing. Most certainly the proposed plan would be dependent upon reasonable good faith for its successful working, but this is only to say what is also true of every human institution. Under the proposed plan there would be a strong likelihood of bettering world conditions. If it is a Utopia, it is a Utopia of a very practical kind.

Such a plan is as yet in the realm of mere speculation. At present the essential thing for each self-respecting, liberty-loving nation to do is to put itself in position to defend its own rights. Recently President Wilson, in his message to Congress, has announced that we are in no danger and will not be in any danger; and ex-President Taft has stated that the awakening of interest in our defenses indicates "mild hysteria." Such utterances show fatuous indifference to the teachings of history. They represent precisely the attitude which a century ago led to the burning of Washington by a small expeditionary hostile force, and to such paralyzing disaster in war as almost to bring about the break-up of the Union. In his message President Wilson justifies a refusal to build up our navy by asking – as if we were discussing a question of pure metaphysics – "When will the experts tell us just what kind of ships we should construct – and when will they be right for ten years together? Who shall tell us now what sort of navy to build?" and actually adds, after posing and leaving unanswered these questions: "I turn away from the subject. It is not new. There is no need to discuss it." Lovers of Dickens who turn to the second paragraph of chapter XI of "Our Mutual Friend" will find this attitude of President Wilson toward preparedness interestingly paralleled by the attitude Mr. Podsnap took in "getting rid of disagreeables" by the use of the phrases, "I don't want to know about them! I refuse to discuss them! I don't admit them!" thus "clearing the world of its most difficult problems by sweeping them behind him. For they affronted him." If during the last ten years England's attitude toward preparedness for war and the up-building of her navy had been determined by statesmanship such as is set forth in these utterances of President Wilson, the island would now be trampled into bloody mire, as Belgium has been trampled. If Germany had followed such advice – or rather no advice – during the last ten years, she would now have been wholly unable so much as to assert her rights anywhere.

Let us immediately make our navy thoroughly efficient; and this can only be done by reversing the policy that President Wilson has followed for twenty-two months. Recently Secretary Daniels has said,

147

as quoted by the press, that he intends to provide for the safety of both the Atlantic and Pacific coasts by dividing our war fleet between the two oceans. Such division of the fleet, having in view the disaster which exactly similar action brought on Russia ten years ago, would be literally a crime against the nation. Neither our foreign affairs nor our naval affairs can be satisfactorily managed when the President is willing to put in their respective departments gentlemen like Messrs. Bryan and Daniels. President Wilson would not have ventured to make either of these men head of the Treasury Department, because he would thereby have offended the concrete interests of American business men. But as Secretary of State and Secretary of the Navy the harm they do is to the country as a whole. No concrete interest is immediately affected; and, as it is only our own common welfare in the future, only the welfare of our children, only the honor and interest of the United States through the generations that are concerned, it is deemed safe to disregard this welfare and to take chances with our national honor and interest.

Chapter XII

Summing Up

"Blessed are the peacemakers," not merely the peace lovers; for action is what makes thought operative and valuable. Above all, the peace prattlers are in no way blessed. On the contrary, only mischief has sprung from the activities of the professional peace prattlers, the ultra-pacificists, who, with the shrill clamor of eunuchs, preach the gospel of the milk and water of virtue and scream that belief in the efficacy of diluted moral mush is essential to salvation.

It seems necessary every time I state my position to guard against the counterwords of wilful folly by reiterating that my disagreement with the peace-at-any-price men, the ultrapacificists, is not in the least because they favor peace. I object to them, first, because they have proved themselves futile and impotent in working for peace, and, second, because they commit what is not merely the capital error but the crime against morality of failing to uphold righteousness as the all-important end toward which we should strive. In actual practice they advocate the peace of unrighteousness just as fervently as they advocate the peace of righteousness. I have as little sympathy as they have for the men who deify mere brutal force, who insist that power justifies wrong-doing, and who declare that there is no such thing as international morality. But the ultrapacificists really play into the hands of these men. To condemn equally might which backs right and might which overthrows right is to render positive service to wrong-doers. It is as if in private life we condemned alike both the policeman and the dynamiter or black-hand kidnapper or white slaver whom he has arrested. To denounce the nation that wages war in self-defense, or from a generous desire to relieve the oppressed, in the same terms in which we denounce war waged in a spirit of greed or wanton folly stands on an exact par with denouncing equally a murderer and the policeman who, at peril of his life and by force of arms, arrests the murderer. In each case the denunciation denotes not loftiness of soul but weakness both of mind and of morals.

In a capital book, by a German, Mr. Edmund von Mach, entitled "What Germany Wants," there is the following noble passage at the outset:

> During the preparation of this book the writer received from his uncle, a veteran army officer living in Dresden, a brief note containing the following laconic record:
>
> "1793, your great-grandfather at Kostheim.
>
> "1815, your grandfather at Liegnitz.
>
> "1870, myself – all severely wounded by French bullets.
>
> "1914, my son, captain in the 6th Regiment of Dragoons.
>
> "Four generations obliged to fight the French!"
>
> When the writer turns to his American friends of French descent, he finds there similar records, and often even greater sorrow, for death has come to many of them. In Europe their families and his have looked upon each other as enemies for generations, while a few years in the clarifying atmosphere of America have made friends of former Frenchmen, Germans, Russians, and Englishmen.
>
> Jointly they pray that the present war may not be carried to such a pass that an early and honorable peace becomes impossible for any one of these great nations. Is it asking too much that America may be vouchsafed in not too distant a future to do for their respective native lands what the American institutions have done for them individually, help them to regard each other at their true worth, unblinded by traditional hatred or fiery passion?

It is in the spirit of this statement that we Americans should act. We are a people different from, but akin, to all the nations of Europe. We should feel a real friendship for each of the contesting powers and a real desire to work so as to secure justice for each. This cannot be done by preserving a tame and spiritless neutrality which treats good and evil on precisely the same basis. Such a neutrality never has enabled and never will enable any nation to do a great work for righteousness.

Our true course should be to judge each nation on its conduct, unhesitatingly to antagonize every nation that does ill as regards the point on which it does ill, and equally without hesitation to act, as cool-headed and yet generous wisdom may dictate, so as disinterestedly to further the welfare of all.

One of the greatest of international duties ought to be the protection of small, highly civilized, well-behaved, and self-respecting states from oppression and conquest by their powerful military neighbors. Such nations as Belgium, Holland, Switzerland, Uruguay, Denmark, Norway, and Sweden play a great and honorable part in the development of civilization. The subjugation of any one of them is a crime against, the destruction of any one of them is a loss to, mankind.

I feel in the strongest way that we should have interfered, at least to the extent of the most emphatic diplomatic protest and at the very outset – and then by whatever further action was necessary – in regard to the violation of the neutrality of Belgium; for this act was the earliest and the most important and, in its consequences, the most ruinous of all the violations and offenses against treaties committed by any combatant during the war. But it was not the only one. The Japanese and English forces not long after violated Chinese neutrality in attacking Kiao-Chau. It has been alleged and not denied that the British ship *Highflyer* sunk the *Kaiser Wilhelm der Grosse* in neutral Spanish waters, this being also a violation of the Hague conventions; and on October 10th the German government issued an official protest about alleged violations of the Geneva convention by the French. Furthermore, the methods employed in strewing portions of the seas with floating mines have been such as to warrant the most careful investigation by any neutral nations which treat neutrality pacts and Hague conventions as other than merely dead letters. Not a few offenses have been committed against our own people.

If, instead of observing a timid and spiritless neutrality, we had lived up to our obligations by taking action in all of these cases without regard to which power it was that was alleged to have done wrong, we would have followed the only course that would both have told for world righteousness and have served our own self-respect. The course actually followed by Messrs. Wilson, Bryan, and Daniels has been to permit our own power for self-defense steadily to diminish while at the same time refusing to do what we were solemnly bound to do in order to protest against wrong and to render some kind of aid to weak nations that had been wronged. Inasmuch as, in the first and greatest and the most ruinous case of violation of neutral rights and of international morality, this nation, under the guidance of Messrs. Wilson and Bryan, kept timid silence and dared not protest, it would be – and is – an act of deliberate bad faith to protest only as regards subsequent and less important violations. Of course, if, as a people, we frankly take the ground that our actions are based upon nothing whatever but our own selfish and short-sighted interest, it is possible to protest only against violations of neutrality that at the moment unfavorably affect our own interests. Inaction is often itself the most offensive form of action; the administration has persistently refused to live up to the solemn national obligations to strive to protect other unoffending nations from wrong; and this conduct adds a peculiar touch of hypocrisy to the action taken at the same time in signing a couple of score of all-inclusive arbitration treaties pretentiously heralded as serving world righteousness. If we had acted as we ought to have acted regarding Belgium we could then with a clear conscience have made effective protest regarding every other case of violation of the rights of neutrals or of offenses committed by the belligerents against one another or against us in violation of the Hague conventions. Moreover, the attitude of the administration has not even placated the powers it was desired to please. Thanks to its action, the United States during the last five months has gained neither the good-will nor the respect of any of the combatants. On the contrary, it has steadily grown rather more disliked and rather less respected by all of them.

In facing a difficult and critical situation, any administration is entitled to a free hand until it has had time to develop the action which it considers appropriate, for often there is more than one way in which it is possible to take efficient action. But when so much time has passed, either without action or with only mischievous action, as gravely to compromise both the honor and the interest of the country, then it becomes a duty for self-respecting citizens to whom their country is dear to speak out. From the very outset I felt that the administration was following a wrong course. But no action of mine could make it take the right course, and there was a possibility that there was some object aside from political advantage in the course followed. I kept silence as long as silence was compatible with regard for the national honor and welfare. I spoke only when it became imperative to speak under penalty of tame acquiescence in tame failure to perform national duty. It has become evident that the administration has had no plan whatever save the dexterous avoidance of all responsibility and therefore of all duty, and the effort to persuade our people as a whole that this inaction was for their interest – combined with other less openly expressed and less worthy efforts of purely political type.

There is therefore no longer any reason for failure to point out that if the President and Secretary of State had been thoroughly acquainted in advance, as of course they ought to have been acquainted, with the European situation, and if they had possessed an intelligent and resolute purpose squarely to meet their heavy responsibilities and thereby to serve the honor of this country and the interest of mankind, they would have taken action on July 29th, 30th, or 31st, certainly not later than August 1st. On such occasions there is a peculiar applicability in the old proverb: Nine tenths of wisdom consists in being wise in time. If those responsible for the management of our foreign affairs had been content to dwell in a world of fact instead of a world of third-rate fiction, they would have understood that at such a time of world crisis it was an unworthy avoidance of duty to fuss with silly little all-inclusive arbitration treaties when the need of the day demanded that they devote all their energies to the terrible problems of the day. They would have known that a German invasion of Switzerland was possible but improbable and a German invasion of Belgium overwhelmingly probable. They would have known that vigorous action by the United States government, taken with such entire good faith as to make it evident that it was in the interest of Belgium and not in the interest of France and England, and that if there was occasion it would be taken against France and England as quickly as against Germany, might very possibly have resulted in either putting a stop to the war or in localizing and narrowly circumscribing its area. It is, of course, possible that the action would have failed of its immediate purpose. But even in that case it cannot be doubted that it would have been efficient as a check upon the subsequent wrongs committed.

Nor was the opportunity for action limited in time. Even if the administration had failed thus to act at the outset of the war, the protests officially made both by the German Emperor and by the Belgian government to the President as to alleged misconduct in the prosecution of the war not only gave him warrant for action but required him to act. Meanwhile, from the moment when the war was declared, it became inexcusable of the administration not to take immediate steps to put the navy into efficient shape, and at least to make our military forces on land more respectable. It is possible not to justify but to explain the action of the administration in using the navy for the sixteen months prior to this war in such a way as greatly to impair its efficiency; for of course when the President selected Mr. Daniels as Secretary of the Navy he showed, on the supposition that he was not indifferent to its welfare, an entire ignorance of what that welfare demanded; and therefore the failure to keep the navy efficient may have been due at first to mere inability to exercise foresight. But with war impending, such failure to exercise foresight became inexcusable. None of the effective fighting craft are of any real use so far as Mexico is concerned. The navy should at once have been assembled in northern waters, either in the Atlantic or the Pacific, and immediate steps taken to bring it to the highest point of efficiency.

It is because I believe our attitude should be one of sincere goodwill toward all nations that I so strongly feel that we should endeavor to work for a league of peace among all nations rather than trust to alliances with any particular group. Moreover, alliances are very shifty and uncertain. Within twenty years England has regarded France as her immediately dangerous opponent; within ten years she has felt that Russia was the one power against which she must at all costs guard herself; and during the same period there have been times when Belgium has hated England with a peculiar fervor. Alliances must be based on self-interest and must continually shift. But in such a world league as that of which we speak and dream, the test would be conduct and not merely selfish interest, and so there would be no shifting of policy.

It is not yet opportune to discuss in detail the exact method by which the nations of the world shall put the collective strength of civilization behind the purpose of civilization to do right, using as an instrumentality for peace such a world league. I have in the last chapter given the bare outline of such a plan. Probably at the outset it would be an absolute impossibility to devise a non-national or purely international police form which would be effective in a great crisis. The prime necessity is that all the great nations should agree in good faith to use their combined warlike strength to coerce any nation, whichever one it may be, that declines to abide the decision of some competent international tribunal.

Our business is to create the beginnings of international order out of the world of nations as these nations actually exist. We do not have to deal with a world of pacificists and therefore we must proceed on the assumption that treaties will never acquire sanctity until nations are ready to seal them with their blood. We are not striving for peace in heaven. That is not our affair. What we were bidden to strive for is "peace on earth and good-will toward men." To fulfil this injunction it is necessary to treat the earth as it is and men as they are, as an indispensable prerequisite to making the earth a better place in which to live and men better fit to live in it. It is inexcusable moral culpability on our part to pretend to carry out this injunction in such fashion as to nullify it; and this we do if we make believe that the earth is what it is not and if our professions of bringing good-will toward men are in actual practice shown to be empty shams. Peace congresses, peace parades, the appointment and celebration of days of prayer for peace, and the like, which result merely in giving the participants the feeling that they have accomplished something and are therefore to be excused from hard, practical work for righteousness, are empty shams. Treaties such as the recent all-inclusive arbitration treaties are worse than empty shams and convict us as a nation of moral culpability when our representatives sign them at the same time that they refuse to risk anything to make good the signatures we have already affixed to the Hague conventions.

Moderate and sensible treaties which mean something and which can and will be enforced mark a real advance for the human race. As has been well said: "It is our business to make no treaties which we are not ready to maintain with all our resources, for every such 'scrap of paper' is like a forged check – an assault on our credit in the world." Promises that are idly given and idly broken represent profound detriment to the morality of nations. Until no promise is idly entered into and until promises that have once been made are kept, at no matter what cost of risk and effort and positive loss, just so long will distrust and suspicion and wrong-doing rack the world. No honest lawyer will hesitate to advise his client against signing a contract either detrimental to his interests or impossible of fulfilment; and the individual who signs such a contract at once makes himself either an object of suspicion to sound-headed men or else an object of derision to all men. One of the stock jokes in the comic columns of the newspapers refers to the man who swears off or takes the pledge, or makes an indefinite number of good resolutions on New Year's Day, and fails to keep his pledge or promise or resolution; this was one of Mark Twain's favorite subjects for derision. The man who continually makes new promises without living up to those he has already made, and who takes pledges which he breaks, is rightly treated as an object for contemptuous fun. The nation which behaves in like manner deserves no higher consideration.

The conduct of President Wilson and Secretary Bryan in signing these all-inclusive treaties at the same time that they have kept silent about the breaking of the Hague conventions has represented the kind of wrong-doing to this nation that would be represented in private life by the conduct of the individuals who sign such contracts as those mentioned. The administration has looked on without a protest while the Hague conventions have been torn up and thrown to the wind. It has watched the paper structure of good-will collapse without taking one step to prevent it; and yet foolish pacificists, the very men who in the past have been most vociferous about international morality, have praised it for this position. The assertion that our neutrality carries with it the obligation to be silent when our own Hague conventions are destroyed represents an active step against the peace of righteousness. The only way to show that our faith in public law was real was to protest against the assault on international morality implied in the invasion of Belgium.

Unless some one at some time is ready to take some chance for the sake of internationalism, that is of international morality, it will remain what it is to-day, an object of derision to aggressive nations. Even if nothing more than an emphatic protest had been made against what was done in Belgium – it is not at this time necessary for me to state exactly what, in my judgment, ought to have been done – the foundations would have been laid for an effective world opinion against international cynicism. Pacificists claim that we have acted so as to preserve the good-will of Europe and to exercise a guiding influence in the settlement of the war. This is an idea which appeals to the thoughtless, for it gratifies our desire to keep out of trouble and also our vanity by the hope that we shall do great things with small difficulty. It may or may not be that the settlement will finally be made by a peace congress in which the President of the United States will hold titular position of headship. But under conditions as they are now the real importance of the President in such a peace congress will be comparable to the real importance of the drum-major when he walks at the head of a regiment. Small boys regard the drum-major as much more important than the regimental commander; and the pacificist grown-ups who applaud peace congresses sometimes show as regards the drum-majors of these congresses the same touching lack of insight which small boys show toward real drum-majors. As a matter of fact, if the United States enters such a congress with nothing but a record of comfortable neutrality or tame acquiescence in violated Hague conventions, plus an array of vague treaties with no relation to actual facts, it will be allowed to fill the position of international drum-major and of nothing more; and even this position it will be allowed to fill only so long as it suits the convenience of the men who have done the actual fighting. The warring nations will settle the issues in accordance with their own strength and position. Under such conditions we shall be treated as we deserve to be treated, as a nation of people who mean well feebly, whose words are not backed by deeds, who like to prattle about both their own strength and their own righteousness, but who are unwilling to run the risks without which righteousness cannot be effectively served, and who are also unwilling to undergo the toil of intelligent and hard-working preparation without which strength when tested proves weakness.

In this world it is as true of nations as of individuals that the things best worth having are rarely to be obtained in cheap fashion. There is nothing easier than to meet in congresses and conventions and pass resolutions in favor of virtue. There is also nothing more futile unless those passing the resolutions are willing to make them good by labor and endurance and active courage and self-denial. Readers of John Hay's poems will remember the scorn therein expressed for those who "resoloot till the cows come home," but do not put effort back of their words. Those who would teach our people that service can be rendered or greatness attained in easy, comfortable fashion, without facing risk, hardship, and difficulty, are teaching what is false and mischievous. Courage, hard work, self-mastery, and intelligent effort are all essential to successful life. As a rule, the slothful ease of life is in inverse proportion to its true success. This is true of the private lives of farmers, business men, and mechanics. It is no less true of the life of the nation which is made up of these farmers, business men, and mechanics.

As yet, as events have most painfully shown, there is nothing to be expected by any nation in a great crisis from anything except its own strength. Under these circumstances it is criminal in the United States not to prepare. Critics have stated that in advocating universal military service on the Swiss plan in this country, I am advocating militarism. I am not concerned with mere questions of terminology. The plan I advocate would be a corrective of every evil which we associate with the name of militarism. It would tend for order and self-respect among our people. Not the smallest evil among the many evils that exist in America is due to militarism. Save in the crisis of the Civil War there has been no militarism in the United States and the only militarist President we have ever had was Abraham Lincoln. Universal service of the Swiss type would be educational in the highest and best sense of the word. In Switzerland, as compared with the United States, there are, relatively to the population, only one tenth the number of murders and of crimes of violence. Doubtless other causes have contributed to this, but doubtless also the intelligent collective training of the Swiss people in habits of obedience, of self-reliance, self-restraint and endurance, of applied patriotism and collective action, has been a very potent factor in producing this good result.

As I have already said, I know of my own knowledge that two nations which on certain occasions were obliged, perhaps as much by our fault as by theirs, to take into account the question of possible war with the United States, planned in such event to seize the Panama Canal and to take and ransom or destroy certain of our great coast cities. They planned this partly in the belief that our navy would intermittently be allowed to become extremely inefficient, just as during the last twenty months it has become inefficient, and partly in the belief that our people are so wholly unmilitary, and so ridden to death on the one hand by foolish pacificists and on the other by brutal materialists whose only God is money, that we would not show ourselves either resolutely patriotic or efficient even in what belated action our utter lack of preparation permitted us to take. I believe that these nations were and are wrong in their estimate of the underlying strength of the American character. I believe that if war did really come both the ultra-pacificists, the peace-at-any-price men, and the merely brutal materialists, who count all else as nothing compared to the gratification of their greed for gain or their taste for ease, for pleasure, and for vacuous excitement, would be driven before the gale of popular feeling as leaves are driven through the fall woods. But such aroused public feeling in the actual event would be wholly inadequate to make good our failure to prepare.

We should in all humility imitate not a little of the spirit so much in evidence among the Germans and the Japanese, the two nations which in modern times have shown the most practical type of patriotism, the greatest devotion to the common weal, the greatest success in developing their economic resources and abilities from within, and the greatest far-sightedness in safeguarding the country against possible disaster from without. In the *Journal of the Military Service Institution* for the months of November and December of the present year will be found a quotation from a Japanese military paper, *The Comrades' Magazine*, which displays an amount of practical good sense together with patriotism and devotion to the welfare of the average man which could well be copied by our people and which is worthy of study by every intelligent American. Germany's success in industrialism has been as extraordinary and noteworthy as her success in securing military efficiency, and fundamentally has been due to the development of the same qualities in the nation.

At present the United States does not begin to get adequate return in the way of efficient preparation for defense from the amount of money appropriated every year. Both the executive and Congress are responsible for this – and of course this means that the permanent and ultimate responsibility rests on the people. It is really less a question of spending more money than of knowing how to get the best results for the money that we do spend. Most emphatically there should be a comprehensive plan both for defense and for expenditure. The best military and naval authorities – not merely the senior officers but the best officers – should be required to produce comprehensive plans for battle-ships, for submarines, for air-ships, for proper artillery, for a more efficient regular army, and for a great popular reserve behind the army. Every useless military post should be forthwith abandoned; and this cannot be done save by getting Congress to accept or reject plans for defense and expenditure in their entirety. If each congressman or senator can put in his special plea for the erection or retention of a military post for non-military reasons, and for the promotion or favoring of some given officer or group of officers also for non-military reasons, we can rest assured that good results can never be obtained. Here, again, what is needed is not plans by outsiders but the insistence by outsiders upon the army and navy officers being required to produce the right plans, being backed up when they do produce the right plans, and being held to a strict accountability for any failure, active or passive, in their duty.

Moreover, these plans must be treated as part of the coherent policy of the nation in international affairs. With a gentleman like Mr. Bryan in the State Department it may be accepted as absolutely certain that we never will have the highest grade of efficiency in the Departments of War and of the Navy. With a gentleman like Mr. Daniels at the head of the navy, it may be accepted as certain that the navy will not be brought to the level of its possible powers. This means that the people as a whole must demand of their leaders that they treat seriously the navy and army and our foreign policy.

The waste in our navy and army is very great. This is inevitable as long as we do not discriminate against the inefficient and as long as we fail to put a premium upon efficiency. When I was President I found out that a very large proportion of the old officers of the army and even of the navy were physically incompetent to perform many of their duties. The public was wholly indifferent on the subject. Congress would not act. As a preliminary, and merely as a preliminary, I established a regulation that before promotion officers should be required to walk fifty miles or ride one hundred miles in three days. This was in no way a sufficient test of an officer's fitness. It merely served to rid the service of men whose unfitness was absolutely ludicrous. Yet in Congress and in the newspapers an extraordinary din was raised against this test on the ground that it was unjust to faithful elderly officers! The pacificists promptly assailed it on the ground that to make the army efficient was a "warlike" act. All kinds of philanthropists, including clergymen and college presidents, wrote me that my action showed not only callousness of heart but also a regrettable spirit of militarism. Any officer who because of failure to come up to the test or for other reasons was put out of the service was certain to receive ardent congressional championship; and every kind of pressure was brought to bear on behalf of the unfit, while hardly the slightest effective championship was given the move from any outside source. This was because public opinion was absolutely uneducated on the subject. In our country the men who in time of peace speak loudest about war are usually the ultrapacificists whose activities have been shown to be absolutely futile for peace, but who do a little mischief by persuading a number of well-meaning persons that preparedness for war is unnecessary.

It is not desirable that civilians, acting independently of and without the help of military and naval advisers, shall prepare minute or detailed plans as to what ought to be done for our national defense. But civilians are competent to advocate plans in outline exactly as I have here advocated them. Moreover, and most important, they are competent to try to make public opinion effective in these matters. A democracy must have proper leaders. But these leaders must be able to appeal to a proper sentiment in the democracy. It is the prime duty of every right-thinking citizen at this time to aid his fellow countrymen to understand the need of working wisely for peace, the folly of acting unwisely for peace, and, above all, the need of real and thorough national preparedness against war.

Former Secretary of the Navy Bonaparte, in one of his admirable articles, in which he discusses armaments and treaties, has spoken as follows:

Indeed, it is so obviously impolitic, on the part of the administration and its party friends, to avow a purpose to keep the people in the dark as to our preparedness (or rather as to our virtually admitted unpreparedness) to protect the national interests, safety, and honor, that a practical avowal of such purpose on their part would seem altogether incredible, but for certain rather notorious facts developed by our experience during the last year and three quarters.

It has gradually become evident, or, at least, probable that the mind (wherever that mind may be located) which determines, or has, as yet, determined, our foreign policy under President Wilson, really relies upon a timid neutrality and innumerable treaties of general arbitration as sufficient to protect us from foreign aggression; and advisedly wishes to keep us virtually unarmed and helpless to defend ourselves, so that a sense of our weakness may render us sufficiently pusillanimous to pocket all insults, to submit to any form of outrage, to resent no provocation, and to abdicate completely and forever the dignity and the duties of a great nation.

In the absence of actual experience, a strong effort of the imagination would be required, at least on the part of the writer, to conceive of anybody's not finding such an outlook for his country utterly intolerable; but incredulity must yield to decisive proof. Even the votaries of this novel cult of cowardice, however, are evidently compelled to recognize that, as yet, they constitute a very small minority among Americans, and, for this reason, they would keep their fellow countrymen, as far as may be practicable, in the dark as to our national weakness and our national dangers; they delight in gagging soldiers and sailors and, to the extent of their power, everybody else who may speak with any authority, and, if they could, would shut out every ray of light which might aid public opinion to see things as they are.

* * *

There is no room for difference as to the utter absurdity of reliance on treaties, no matter how solemn or with whomsoever made, as substitutes for proper armaments to assure the national safety; Belgium's fate stares in the face any one who should even dream of this. Her neutrality was established and guaranteed, not by one treaty but by several treaties, not by one power but by all the powers; yet she has been completely ruined because she relied upon these treaties, refused to violate them herself and tried, in good faith, to fulfil the obligations they imposed on her.

For any public man, with this really terrible object-lesson before his eyes, to seriously ask us to believe that arbitration treaties or Hague tribunals or anything else within that order of ideas can be trusted to take the place of preparation impeaches either his sincerity or his sanity, and impeaches no less obviously the common sense of his readers or hearers.

A nation unable to protect itself may have to pay a frightful price nowadays as a penalty for the misfortune of weakness; the Belgians may be, in a measure, consoled for their misfortune by the world's respect and sympathy; in the like case, we should be further and justly punished by the world's unbounded and merited contempt, for our weakness would be the fruit of our own ignominious cowardice and incredible folly.

Secretary Garrison in his capital report says that if our outlying possessions are even insufficiently manned our mobile home army will consist of less than twenty-five thousand men, only about twice the size of the police force of New York City. Yet, in the face of this, certain newspaper editors, college presidents, pacificist bankers and, I regret to say, certain clergymen and philanthropists enthusiastically champion the attitude of President Wilson and Mr. Bryan in refusing to prepare for war. As one of them put it the other day: "The way to prevent war is not to fight." Luxembourg did not fight! Does this gentleman regard the position of Luxembourg at this moment as enviable? China has not recently fought. Does the gentleman think that China's position is in consequence a happy one? If advisers of this type, if these college presidents and clergymen and editors of organs of culture and the philanthropists who give this advice spoke only for themselves, if the humiliation and disgrace were to come only on them, no one would have a right to object. They have servile souls; and if they chose serfdom of the body for themselves only, it would be of small consequence to others. But, unfortunately, their words have a certain effect upon this country; and that effect is intolerably evil. Doubtless it is the influence of these men which is largely responsible for the attitude of the President. The President attacks preparedness in the name of anti-militarism. The preparedness we advocate is that of Switzerland, the least militaristic of countries. Autocracy may use preparedness for the creation of an aggressive and provocative militarism that invites and produces war; but in a democracy preparedness means security against aggression and the best guarantee of peace. The President in his message has in effect declared that his theory of neutrality, which is carried to the point of a complete abandonment of the rights of innocent small nations, and his theory of non-preparedness, which is carried to the point of gross national inefficiency, are both means for securing to the United States a leading position in bringing about peace. The position he would thus secure would be merely that of drum-major at the peace conference; and he would do well to remember that if the peace that is brought about should result in leaving Belgium's wrongs unredressed and turning Belgium over to Germany, in enthroning militarism as the chief factor in the modern world, and in consecrating the violation of treaties, then the United States, by taking part in such a conference, would have rendered an evil service to mankind.

At present our navy is in wretched shape. Our army is infinitesimal. This large, rich republic is far less efficient from a military standpoint than Switzerland, Holland, or Denmark. In spite of the fact that the officers and enlisted men of our navy and army offer material on the whole better than the officers and men of any other navy or army, these two services have for so many years been neglected by Congress, and during the last two years have been so mishandled by the administration, that at the present time an energetic and powerful adversary could probably with ease drive us not only from the Philippines but from Hawaii, and take possession of the Canal and Alaska. If invaded by a serious army belonging to some formidable Old World empire, we would be for many months about as helpless as China; and, as nowadays large armies can cross the ocean, we might be crushed beyond hope of recuperation inside of a decade. Yet those now at the head of public affairs refuse themselves to face facts and seek to mislead the people as to the facts.

President Wilson is, of course, fully and completely responsible for Mr. Bryan. Mr. Bryan appreciates this and loyally endeavors to serve the President and to come to his defense at all times. As soon as President Wilson had announced that there was no need of preparations to defend ourselves, because we loved everybody and everybody loved us and because our mission was to spread the gospel of peace, Mr. Bryan came to his support with hearty enthusiasm and said: "The President knows that if this country needed a million men, and needed them in a day, the call would go out at sunrise and the sun would go down on a million men in arms." One of the President's stanchest newspaper adherents lost its patience over this utterance and remarked: "More foolish words than these of the Secretary of State were never spoken by mortal man in reply to a serious argument." However, Mr. Bryan had a good precedent, although he probably did not know it. Pompey, when threatened by Cæsar, and told that his side was unprepared, responded that he had only to "stamp his foot" and legions would spring from the ground. In the actual event, the "stamping" proved as effectual against Cæsar as Mr. Bryan's "call" would under like circumstances. I once heard a Bryanite senator put Mr. Bryan's position a little more strongly than it occurred to Mr. Bryan himself to put it. The senator in question announced that we needed no regular army, because in the event of war "ten million freemen would spring to arms, the equals of any regular soldiers in the world." I do not question the emotional or oratorical sincerity either of Mr. Bryan or of the senator. Mr. Bryan is accustomed to performing in vacuo; and both he and President Wilson, as regards foreign affairs, apparently believe they are living in a world of two dimensions, and not in the actual workaday world, which has three dimensions. This was equally true of the senator in question. If the senator's ten million men sprang to arms at this moment, they would have at the outside some four hundred thousand modern rifles to which to spring. Perhaps six hundred thousand more could spring to squirrel pieces and fairly good shotguns. The remaining nine million men would have to "spring" to axes, scythes, hand-saws, gimlets, and similar arms. As for Mr. Bryan's million men who would at sunset respond under arms to a call made at sunrise, the suggestion is such a mere rhetorical flourish that it is not worthy even of humorous treatment; a high-school boy making web a statement in a theme would be marked zero by any competent master. But it is an exceedingly serious thing, it is not in the least a humorous thing, that the man making such a statement should be the chief adviser of the President in international matters, and should hold the highest office in the President's gift.

Nor is Mr. Bryan in any way out of sympathy with President Wilson in this matter. The President, unlike Mr. Bryan, uses good English and does not say things that are on their face ridiculous. Unfortunately, his cleverness of style and his entire refusal to face facts apparently make him believe that he really has dismissed and done away with ugly realities whenever he has uttered some pretty phrase about them. This year we are in the presence of a crisis in the history of the world. In the terrible whirlwind of war all the great nations of the world, save the United States and Italy, are facing the supreme test of their history. All of the pleasant and alluring but futile theories of the pacificists, all the theories enunciated in the peace congresses of the past twenty years, have vanished at the first sound of the drumming guns. The work of all the Hague conventions, and all the arbitration treaties, neutrality treaties, and peace treaties of the last twenty years has been swept before the gusts of war like withered leaves before a November storm. In this great crisis the stern and actual facts have shown that the fate of each nation depends not in the least upon any elevated international aspirations to which it has given expression in speech or treaty, but on practical preparation, on intensity of patriotism, on grim endurance, and on the possession of the fighting edge. Yet, in the face of all this, the President of the United States sends in a message dealing with national defense, which is filled with prettily phrased platitudes of the kind applauded at the less important type of peace congress, and with sentences cleverly turned to conceal from the average man the fact that the President has no real advice to give, no real policy to propose. There is just one point as to which he does show real purpose for a tangible end. He dwells eagerly upon the hope that we may obtain "the opportunity to counsel and obtain peace in the world" among the warring nations and adjures us not to jeopardize this chance (for the President to take part in the peace negotiations) by at this time making any preparations for self-defense. In effect, we are asked not to put our own shores in defensible condition lest the President may lose the chance to be at the head of the congress which may compose the differences of Europe. In effect, he asks us not to build up the navy, not to provide for an efficient citizen army, not to get ammunition for our guns and torpedoes for our torpedo-tubes, lest somehow or other this may make the President of the United States an unacceptable mediator between Germany and Great Britain! It is an honorable ambition for the President to desire to be of use in bringing about peace in Europe; but only on condition that the peace thus brought is the peace of right-eousness, and only on condition that he does not sacrifice this country's vital interests for a clatter of that kind of hollow applause through which runs an undertone of sinister jeering. He must not sacrifice to this ambition the supreme interest of the American people. Nor must he believe that the possibility of his being umpire will have any serious effect on the terrible war game that is now being played; the outcome of the game will depend upon the prowess of the players. No gain will come to our nation, or to any other nation, if President Wilson permits himself to be deluded concerning the part the United States may take in the promotion of European peace.

Peace in Europe will be made by the warring nations. They and they alone will in fact determine the terms of settlement. The United States may be used as a convenient means of getting together; but that is all. If the nations of Europe desire peace and our assistance in securing it, it will be because they have fought as long as they will or can. It will not be because they regard us as having set a spiritual example to them by sitting idle, uttering cheap platitudes, and picking up their trade, while they have poured out their blood like water in support of the ideals in which, with all their hearts and souls, they believe. For us to assume superior virtue in the face of the war-worn nations of the Old World will not make us more acceptable as mediators among them. Such self-consciousness on our part will not impress the nations who have sacrificed and are sacrificing all that is dearest to them in the world, for the things that they believe to be the noblest in the world. The storm that is raging in Europe at this moment is terrible and evil; but it is also grand and noble. Untried men who live at ease will do well to remember that there is a certain sublimity even in Milton's defeated archangel, but none whatever in the spirits who kept neutral, who remained at peace, and dared side neither with hell nor with heaven. They will also do well to remember that when heroes have battled together, and have wrought good and evil, and when the time has come out of the contest to get all the good possible and to prevent as far as possible the evil from being made permanent, they will not be influenced much by the theory that soft and short-sighted outsiders have put themselves in better condition to stop war abroad by making themselves defenseless at home.